OLD COTTAGES

FARM-HOUSES ETC. IN

THE COTSWOLD DISTRICT

A GROUP OF COTTAGES, BIBURY, GLOS.

OLD COTTAGES
FARM-HOUSES, AND
OTHER STONE BUILDINGS

IN .

THE COTSWOLD DISTRICT

EXAMPLES OF MINOR DOMESTIC ARCHITECTURE IN

GLOUCESTERSHIRE, OXFORDSHIRE,
NORTHANTS, WORCESTERSHIRE, &c.,

ILLUSTRATED ON ONE HUNDRED COLLOTYPE PLATES
FROM PHOTOGRAPHS SPECIALLY TAKEN BY

W. GALSWORTHY DAVIE

WITH AN INTRODUCTORY ACCOUNT
OF THE ARCHITECTURE OF THE DISTRICT
ACCOMPANIED BY NOTES AND SKETCHES

By E. GUY DAWBER, Architect

LONDON :

B. T. BATSFORD 94 HIGH HOLBORN

1905

BUTLER & TANNER,
THE SELWOOD PRINTING WORKS
FROME, AND LONDON.

PREFACE

THE success which attended the publication of the volume entitled " *Old Cottages and Farm Houses in Kent and Sussex* " encouraged the publisher, in fulfilment of a promise made in the Preface of that work, to follow it by the issue of similar volumes dealing with the minor domestic buildings of other counties; and it is not surprising that he should have decided to devote one of these to the delightfully characteristic work of the Cotswolds.

This district contains some of the most typical stone buildings in England, and they illustrate in a wonderful manner the methods adopted by the old builders in producing most pleasing effects by the employment of one single material. Amongst them are some of the most noteworthy houses in the country, celebrated equally from an historic and a picturesque point of view; but although these are outside the scope of this work, the smaller buildings dealt with in it show in their detail and construction the same high standard of work and design.

Year by year the public show an increasing appreciation of the artistic qualities of the domestic buildings of England, and this neighbourhood, containing some of the most beautiful examples to be found, will appeal to all lovers of the picturesque in architecture.

Mr. W. Galsworthy Davie has taken the charming series of photographs, showing the special characteristics of the Cotswold style, which although resembling in its main outlines similar work in other parts of the country, here exemplifies in the greatest possible degree the perfect adaptability of material to design.

The descriptive notes, and the illustrations accompanying them are the result of many years of personal study and knowledge of the locality, and although they do not pretend in any way to have exhausted the subject, it is hoped, they may be helpful and interesting alike to the architect and such artists and amateurs as take an interest in these matters.

E. GUY DAWBER.

22, BUCKINGHAM STREET,
   ADELPHI, LONDON,
      December, 1904.

ALPHABETICAL LIST OF PLATES

ARRANGED UNDER NAMES OF TOWNS AND VILLAGES

vii

LIST OF ILLUSTRATIONS IN THE TEXT

xi

Old Cottages, Farm-houses, etc., in the Cotswold District

A MONGST the Cotswold hills are to be found examples of domestic architecture, as characteristic as in any other part of England, and although perhaps they do not rank in importance with larger or more pretentious edifices, they possess a singular interest and quiet charm of their own.

The cottages, like the manor houses, the churches and farm-buildings, are all built of the native stone, and all are gabled and picturesque. Perhaps nowhere is there any architecture more perfect in its simplicity and grace than that found in these old English villages.

The houses and hamlets form a more or less distinctive group, and are of great value as showing how simple and truthful building, in the hands of rustic craftsmen and designers, without outside influence, may develop an almost traditional style.

Just as the various phases of architecture have been classified into so-called periods, so with this essentially local type of the Cotswolds, which is in reality a product of evolution, growing out of the inherited knowledge of the wants which the builders had to satisfy, and of the natural material at their disposal. In the Middle Ages, and down to the eighteenth century, architecture, or building, as it is better called, was always influenced by local conditions, and the character of work was much the same all over the country; while such cosmopolitan methods as we adopt to-day were quite unknown.

From the earliest days the Cotswold hills were notable as pasture for sheep, which roamed the downs that spread in almost unbroken succession from the Severn to the Thames. As far back as the twelfth century wool was one of our staple articles of export, being sold to Italy and Flanders.

English wool, and that from the Cotswold districts in particular, was esteemed beyond any other, and before we began the manufacture of woollen goods, we exported so much unwrought wool, that the breeding and feeding of sheep was the general occupation, and it is owing to this that many towns and villages, long since fallen to decay, were once prosperous and wealthy.

This prosperity led to the great era of church building throughout Gloucestershire and Northamptonshire, when so many noble buildings, such as Northleach, Cirencester, Burford, etc., were erected by the pious munificence of the wealthy merchants of the staple. It also brought fortunes to the local " Woolmen," as they were called, and an excellent subsistence to hundreds of their workpeople; indeed, it is not too much to say that it is due to their large trade in wool that the small towns and villages, scattered about these hills, are so full of finely built and beautiful houses.

Centuries ago the Cotswolds were one great sheep-walk from end to end, and what with the wool from his sheep, and the grain from his fields, the Cotswold farmer was well-to-do. But now, alas! those times are no more, and the great barns stand empty, or are allowed to fall into ruins; but they speak very eloquently of the days when this district was one of the wealthiest and most prosperous in all England.

The country at first sight seems wild and bare. The great stretches of upland, chill and oppress the casual visitor with a sense of loneliness and melancholy, and perhaps it is only those who live day by day amongst its rolling hills that appreciate and love its beauties, for the Cotswolds possess a distinctive character of their own, and are unlike any other part of England. The richness of the colour of the soil, the depth of tone in the foliage, and the wonderful deep purples and blues of the hills, all combine to make pictures that appeal to all lovers of English rural scenery.

Geologically these hills form a portion of the great belt of limestones, which extends across England from the Dorsetshire coast to between Filey and Scarborough. To architects in particular the whole formation is of unusual interest, as within these limits are found almost all the building limestones used in England. The hills form an elevated tableland or plateau some 800 to 1,200 feet above sea level, with a fairly steep escarpment facing west, and overlooking the valley of the Severn. This escarpment was perhaps a cliff range overhanging an arm of the sea, but the tableland behind has been cut into valleys by frost, rain, and streams, and swept completely bare of the gravels which lie so thick in the valleys beneath.

The various strata which dip slightly to the S.E. and E., comprise the whole of the Oolite series, a vast mass of more or less continuous beds of limestone, separated by partings of clay. These are all of marine origin and enclose, in places, great amounts of shelly matter; such as beds of oysters, and reefs of coral. The series begins with the Inferior Oolitic limestones, which stretch from Bridport northward to Beaminster and Sherborne, and broaden out on to the flat-topped Cotswold hills east of Cheltenham. These are succeeded by a band of the clayey substance known as Fuller's earth, which, forming a water-bearing zone amongst the hills, supplies the numerous springs found on all sides.

The great or Bath Oolite has at its base the well-known Stonesfield slate, which splits into the coarse fissile slabs, commonly used for roofing. The middle and lower beds give the best stone for building purposes; soft when first quarried, but possessing the well-known property of hardening with exposure.

The stone is usually quarried from about April to October, after which the quarries are closed for the winter months. It is generally obtained by clearing away the upper layers of inferior stone and loose brash, though sometimes it is mined for, as most of the Bath stones are. When first quarried it is rather yellow in tone, but becomes bleached by exposure, and after a time turns to all manner of rich colours, and is quickly covered with lichens, for which it seems to have a peculiar attraction. It is an admirable weather stone, as much old work in the district testifies.

Nearly every village at one time had its local quarry, though many of these have for years been unworked, and it is doubtless owing to their proximity to excellent stone, and the ease with which it could be obtained, that the larger towns like Painswick, Northleach, Burford, Campden and many others grew so rapidly and prospered. Much of the stone used in building St. Paul's Cathedral came from quarries close to Burford, and in that church there is a marble tablet to the memory of Christopher Kempster, who was employed as master mason. These quarries, still called Christopher's or Kitt's quarries, lie a little to the south-west of Burford, and near to them is a large stone house bearing the inscription, " Christopher Kempster built this in 1698."

Owing to the nature of the formation of the hills, the whole
district is essentially a stone one, and all the buildings are constructed of the local limestone, which lies everywhere within a
few feet of the surface. It is doubtless to this, together with the
isolated positions of the villages and hamlets, cut off in many cases
from the main arteries of traffic, that we owe their preservation
to-day, and as stone was practically the only material available, we
cannot but admire the ingenious way in which the old builders
adapted it in their work.

Generally speaking we do not in this district find much domestic work of an earlier date than the close of the sixteenth century, and the bulk of the essentially traditional Cotswold style
ranges from that time to 1700. Perhaps this may be attributed
to the fact that during this period there were more resident gentry
in the country than at any other, and they depended more or
less for their livelihood on the produce of their estates. They
therefore encouraged building, both amongst themselves and the
tenants and inhabitants of their properties, and did much to influence the taste of the time.

During the reign of Queen Anne, when the commercial classes
became such a power in the country, owing to the great expan-
sion of English trade, and fortunes were quickly made, many of
the old Royalist families, who had suffered first by the Civil War,
and then by the reckless extravagance of the Restoration, were
forced to sell their estates. The wealthy merchants bought them
up and expended money in either building new houses for themselves, or in adding to and altering the old ones, but though this
latter phase of work is particularly interesting, it stands in a category by itself, and cannot be called so essentially a Cotswold style
as that of the seventeenth century.

It is doubtful too whether these people, having no ancestral interest in their purchases, did not somewhat neglect the village social life, for during the eighteenth century and even in later years, when the labouring classes became very poor, it was no uncommon occurrence for them to be turned out of their villages, and their cottages pulled down, so that they should not become a burden on the landowners. This in a great measure accounts for the lack of cottage building between the end of the seventeenth century and the middle of the nineteenth.

Broadly speaking the recognized Cotswold type belongs to the period between 1580 and 1690. It was a thoroughly common-sense style of building, based on tradition handed down through generations of village craftsmen, and it remained without change for nearly a century. The main bulk of the buildings were without doubt erected by local men, and without any external aid, for we find the same methods adopted, with but slight local variations, many miles apart. It was a style that was gradually evolved : at first retaining a few links with the so-called Perpendicular work of the preceding century, but slowly shaking these off, until in the course of some few years it settled down to be the traditional work of the day, the vernacular of building in which the craftsman expressed his ideas.

It is no idle plea to urge that this phase of English domestic architecture, although of a humbler sort, merits as much attention and careful study as that of our larger houses and ecclesiastical buildings, for these cottages were built to be lived in by the dwellers of these country villages, and belong to a type of house-building and craftsmanship quite unknown to us to-day.

Occasionally the individuality of the craftsman shows itself in the way of quaint finials, or some delicate wrought iron work to the doors or windows; small touches that give a charm and vitality to his work.

In these cosmopolitan days the use of railways and cheap means of transit have almost obliterated the older crafts, and the advent of bricks and mortar, corrugated iron and foreign timber, is very rapidly driving the local materials and methods of building out of use. This cannot be sufficiently deplored, for apart from its effect upon the employment of labour, it is a matter of serious import that the old handicrafts, which made this country so pre-eminently beautiful, are dying out. The total lack of encouragement given to workers in these simple trades, and the introduction of methods of building quite at variance with those indigenous to the country, combined with the enforcement of restrictive Building Byelaws, are bound in the course of a few years to have a disastrous effect, even if they have not done so already.

In the districts with which we are dealing, it is now a somewhat rare occurrence to find new cottages built with local materials; if they are so it is chiefly by people who have at heart the old traditions, and therefore resist new and strange innovations.

This beautiful type of building, so simple and so strong, and which is as worthy of retention and preservation as any other either in this country or abroad, has never been appreciated at its real value, and buildings both great and small are either allowed to fall into a state of hopeless ruin, or, which is almost worse, to suffer such " restoration " as to render them quite unrecognizable.

Of course we must recollect that the builders of these houses had none of the difficulties to contend with that are ever present to-day. Drainage and sanitation were practically unknown in the way we understand them; water supply and the consequent introduction of pipes inside the house, together with the complication of modern requirements and the over elaboration of planning, were non-existent, so that, when examined in detail they are found to be simple both in plan and arrangement. The absence of small outbuildings, which detract from the restfulness of the main house, all contributed towards the desired effect, as in the farmhouse at Willersey, illustrated on Plate v.

More than anything else the sense of proportion in these houses is the one thing that produces so much of their charm. It is always correct, there is never a false note, for these old builders seem to have understood intuitively the exact relation of voids and solids, of heights and widths, and in a quiet and unpretentious way their houses are almost perfect as specimens of village crafts-manship and building. An admirable example of this type is shown in the Rectory at Coln Roger (Plate xc).

There was no striving after any eccentricities or unnecessary embellishment ; what was good enough for their fathers was good enough for them, and there are villages with houses dating and ranging from the end of the sixteenth to well into the eighteenth century precisely similar in detail, showing how thoroughly these people were imbued with one idea of building.

It may be thought that these villages and country towns are all of a stereotyped pattern and somewhat monotonous, but nothing could be farther from this in reality, as a glance through the illustrations will show, for though there is a repetition of certain forms and features, and we recognize at once that every detail is familiar, yet it is this very similarity of idea permeating the whole of the district during this period that gives such a broad and dignified character to the work (compare for example Plates xxx and lxxii).

The houses were mostly placed in such positions as would

shelter them from exposure to the weather, and give ready access to such roads as then existed. This however was by no means always the case. Apparently no attention was paid to the question of aspect, as to whether the position commanded good views— indeed many of the sites seem particularly ill chosen, lying low, or close to streams, but this last point, in the case of the houses in the Painswick and Stroud valleys, was necessary for the carrying on of trade. Some illustrations of this type are given on Plates lxxiv, lxxxvii and xc.

It is a mistake to suppose, as many people do, that the work of these old time builders was always sound and constructional, and to hold it up as an example to us of to-day, for although they built according to their idea of what was truthful, much of what they did we must perforce condemn now.

Their walls, for instance, though thick and solid in appearance, were often merely an inner and outer shell, filled with rubbish and small stones, which had little or no cohesive properties and consequently could not withstand any settlements, and suffered severely from the effects of wet and frost.

Many of the houses were erected without any foundations, and in some cases the builders never even troubled to remove the turf, but began their walls directly from the surface of the ground.

An eaves gutter, or downspout to carry off the rain was absolutely unknown in a Cotswold house, and the water running directly off the roof, was either blown against the walls, or dripped to the ground, thus accounting for the decayed and worn condition of the base of the walls.

In some of the houses having an occasional parapet and lead gutter, the water emptied itself through a stone gurgoyle, projecting some two or three feet from the wall, a system nearly as bad as the former one, for instead of the water being distributed evenly around the house, it was here collected into a larger volume, which perhaps did greater damage to the building.

The use of lead for any purpose, except window glazing, was in these smaller houses evidently unknown, as a lead head or downspout is never found except in large and important buildings. The wooden V-shaped eaves gutter, and square down pipes, were first used when the necessity became apparent for some means of getting rid of the water, and it is only during the last century that these have been superseded by the iron ones now more or less universal.

No doubt a great deal of the charm of these old houses is due to the fact that they were nearly always self-contained. An admirable example is shown in the cottage by the Cross at Stanton (Plate xxviii). The eaves projected without any gutters or spouting, the breadth of wall surface was unbroken by the vertical lines of down pipes, which cut all modern buildings into strips, and such things as ventilation pipes and sanitary monstrosities being then unknown.

When the houses were built on sloping sites advantage was nearly always taken of it, to cleverly arrange some of the rooms on a lower level and by means of terraces and steps add to the picturesque appearance of the buildings—but unfortunately these lower rooms, owing to wet and damp, are now almost unusable except as store places (see Plates xvi, xxvii, xciv).

As the rooms had outer walls on each side, on the ground floors particularly, and windows in them, they were always cheerful and sunny, but with regard to the bedrooms it was different.

At this period—the seventeenth century—it was for some strange reason thought injurious to sleep in rooms facing the sun, so most of the original rooms faced north and east, opening off a passage, or else out of each other.

The stairs generally ascended in the middle of the house, direct into a room and, as Mr. Baring Gould says in his " *Old Country Life*," "At the head of the stairs slept the master and his wife, and all the rooms tenanted by the rest of the household were accessible only through that. The daughters of the house and maidservants lay in rooms on one side, say the right, with the maids in those most distant ; those of the men lay on the left, the sons of the house nearest the chamber of the master and the serving men furthest off."

This arrangement of rooms opening out of each other, on a

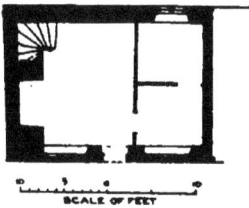

FIG. 1. PLAN OF COTTAGE
AT ICCOMB, GLOS.

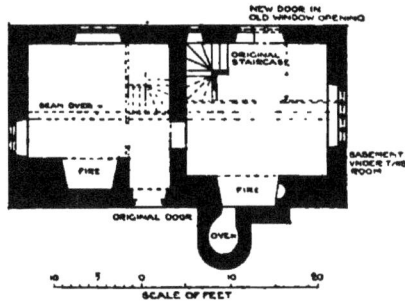

FIG. 2.   PLAN OF COTTAGE AT SNOWS-
HILL (*see* also Plate xxvii).

somewhat simplified scale, is frequently met with to-day, though as a rule an additional staircase gives access to the servants' quarters, from the kitchen below, but the great length of many of the houses shows that the custom must have been universal, as illustrated in Plates v and l.

If we look at the plans of any of these small houses, the first thing that strikes us is the absolute simplicity, not to say baldness, of their arrangement (*see* Figs. 1, 2, 3). The bulk of them have now been converted into two or more separate dwellings, and though many of the later alterations appear at a first glance to have entirely changed the original plan, it is quite easy to reconstruct it. As single houses they consisted of two or three rooms on the ground floor, one, perhaps the living room, being rather larger than the others (*see* Figs. 1, 2, 3). In arrangement these houses carried on the medieval tradition of the one general living and sleeping room, with the " solar " opening off it, for beyond the actual rooms themselves there was nothing; no store cupboards, larders, or conveniences of any description, and everything was contained within the four outer walls.

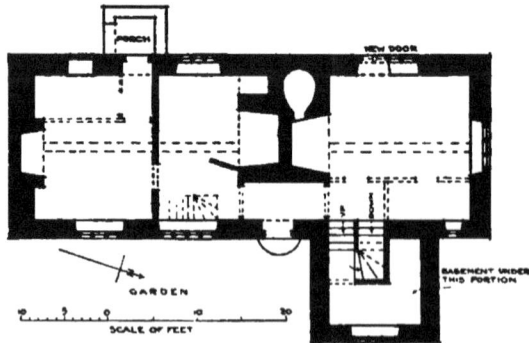

FIG. 3.   PLAN OF COTTAGE AT ASTON SUBEDGE.

They were always planned one room in thickness, (*see* Fig. 4), so that they could be roofed in a single span, and the invariable width is from 16 to 18 feet. When more accommodation was needed, they were made L, E, or H shaped, with a central block and projecting wings, but however large the house, always retaining the single span roof.

Another characteristic, noticeable in each room, is the large fireplace, which gives a greater suggestion of comfort and warmth than almost any other structural feature. It was the spot around which the family would cluster after the day's work in the fields or at the loom, was done, and where the meals were cooked. Most of these fireplaces are very large, as a comparison with the plans will show—frequently 6 feet and upwards in width (*see* Figs. 3 and 4). They were not high—about 4 to 5 feet being the average, and the head was either formed of large stones, shaped as a flat four centred arch, or spanned with a plain lintol of oak. Wood was the usual fuel, burnt on the stone hearth, and pots and kettles were hung from the iron hinged trivet, fixed in one of the innermost angles.

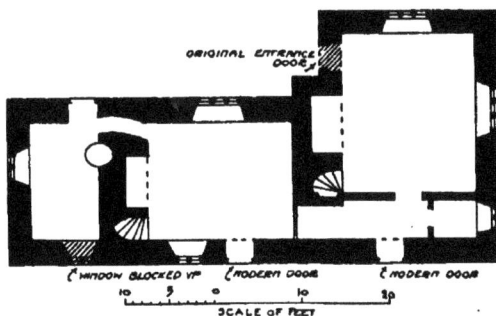

FIG. 4.   PLAN OF COTTAGE AT CHEDWORTH.

Sometimes we find the flat iron ovens standing on the stone hearth, and on the top of these the fire is laid. These ovens are about 2 feet square and 7 or 8 inches deep, placed between small projecting stone piers, with moulded caps, and between these again is the iron fireback. These latter are found in many old houses doubtless owing to their proximity to the coal and iron fields of the Forest of Dean, but few have any great merit, unless it be that of plainness, and none show the exquisite workmanship of the Kent and Sussex examples. The bread oven, in which the faggots were burned, generally opened out of one side of the fireplace, and was sometimes built in the thickness of the wall, or else jutting out in the form of a semicircle with a small roof over it as in the house at Snowshill (*see* Fig. 4 and Plate xxvi). On one or both sides of the fireplace, inside the ingle, a seat was often arranged, in the thickness of the masonry. This consisted of a hollowed out recess, with a stone or wooden bottom, just wide enough for a person to sit down in comfortably, and arched above the head. Some few inches up on each side there were small places

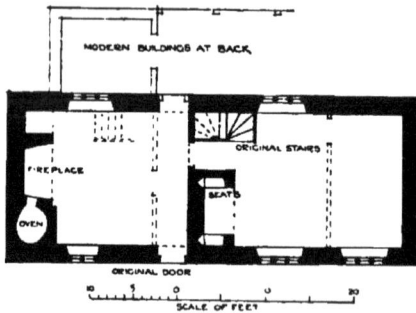

FIG. 5.   COTTAGE AT THE CROSS, STANTON.

hollowed out to take the elbows, or else to stand a glass or cup upon, as in the cottage at Stanton (*see* Fig. 5). Sometimes little cupboards were fitted in on either side of the fireplace as receptacles for food, or pipes and tobacco, as at Medford house (*see* Fig. 80), and occasionally we find small windows behind the seats to light the ingle, but as a rule there are none.

Though their close proximity to the fire has its drawbacks, yet these warm seats are much coveted corners, and in the village inns to-day one frequently sees the old labourers putting up willingly with smarting eyes and general discomfort rather than shift their places.

When these houses were built reading was not much in vogue, and light was not wanted for that purpose. The women of the household evidently did not use the chimney corners for sewing in, owing to the smoke, and doubtless they were chiefly occupied by the men and children. These old ingle nooks, the real genuine article, usually have a large tapering flue carried straight up and open to the sky above. They doubtless smoked exceedingly, as the blackened ceilings show, but as doors and windows fitted badly and draughts must have been abundant, a little smoke more or less could have been of no great consequence!

With the exception of the internal fireplaces and chimney-breasts it is seldom that the rooms are divided by stone walls; the partitions were generally made of strong oak framing, filled in with lath and plaster, or panelled with oak.

The smaller buildings therefore, unless the chimney stack happened to be inside the house, had practically no lateral tie, and this is one of the reasons why so many houses are found with their walls out of plumb, the weight of the roof having thrust them out of the perpendicular.

The floors were carried on joists from wall to wall, or more frequently resting on beams, placed centrally in the rooms without any regard to the positions of the windows and fireplaces, over which they happened to come.   .

These floors, in the cottages, were generally of unsquared joists of timber, often with the bark left on, laid some few inches apart and packed in between with a mixture of clay and chopped straw on interlacing hazel sticks. Underneath the ceiling was plastered, with the floor above either laid with oak boards or else finished with a smooth cement face. Sometimes in the better class houses, the joists were squared and moulded, as at Broadway (Fig. 6), and showed as an open ceiling below.

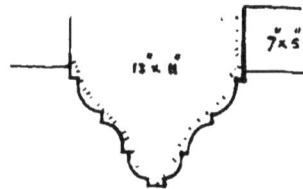

FIG. 6.   BEAM IN CEILING AT BROADWAY.

In the smaller houses it will be seen that the ground floor

rooms are very much alike in size (*see* Fig. 7). In the seventeenth and eighteenth centuries, spinning and weaving formed one of the

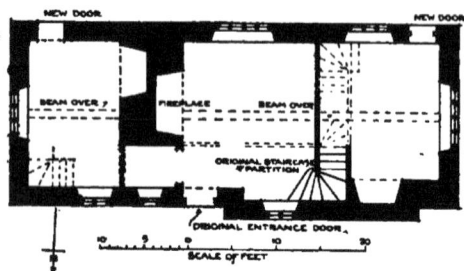

FIG. 7. PLAN OF COTTAGE AT STANTON.

occupations of many of the inhabitants. The spinning wheel converted the wool into worsted, which again was woven into cloth; this of course was some years before the great mills in the Stroud valley mono-polized the bulk of the industry.

The hand-looms have long since disappeared, but the spinning wheels are even now sometimes found amongst the forgotten lumber of the oldest houses, and in the villages around Campden there still exist a few old people who can call to mind hand-looms being used in the cottages.

The walls of the houses which are always of stone throughout, are never less than 18 inches, and often considerably more than 2 feet in thickness. They are composed of rubble stone laid in rather thin layers, or in thicker courses of roughly dressed ashlar, the character of the walling depending in a great measure on the way in which the stone comes from the quarry. Where the stone is only obtained in large blocks the walling is built either of roughly-squared pieces, with regular coursed joints, as in the illustration of the farmhouse at Stanton, (Plate i), or at Laverton, (Plate xxxiv), or else the window dressings and angle quoins are of pieces of dressed stone and the general walling built of random rubble as in the grocer's shop at Colley Weston, (Plate xxix), or of coursed rubble as shown in the illustration of the farmhouse, at Gretton,

(Plate xv), and the cottages at Bibury (Plate lxx). It is therefore easy to tell at a glance from the character of the walling the nature of the stone found in the local quarries.

In many cases in the better class work, this ashlar is carefully dressed and laid square on the beds and upright joints, as in the illustration of the almshouses and market hall at Campden, (Plates x and xi), but this was a costly method of building and is not often met with in the smaller houses.

In the districts where the stone is not found in block, but comes out in thin layers of from 2 to 6 inches thick, the type of walling is again quite different, for here the stone is laid in courses almost as it comes from the quarry, on its natural bed, and the only dressed stone that is used is that to the angles and around the doors and windows—as seen in the illustrations at Harringworth in North-ants, (Plate xii), and Little Rissington and Chedworth in Glouces-tershire (Plate xvi).

In many cases, especially in the eighteenth century, when wooden windows came into use, the ordinary walling stone was built around them, without any dressings at all—as in the illus-trations from Finstock (Plate xvii) and Ducklington (Plate xix) in Oxfordshire.

In quite unpretentious buildings the stone was built in the walls, without any attempt to dress the face, beyond knocking off the projections with the hammer as the stones were laid, and the angle quoins were roughly dressed or scabbled with the mason's axe.

In Northamptonshire we find a pleasant variety in the treat-ment of the walling, where alternate layers of red ironstone are interspersed with the limestone, as in Plates xx, xxi and xxii. This ironstone is found in its greatest thickness in the neighbourhood of Northampton, and is quarried largely at Duston, Blisworth, etc.

Where the stone was got out of large blocks, it had either to be axed square on the face and the beds, or else carefully dressed with the chisel, but in whatever manner worked it was always laid with wide and generous mortar joints.

In many of the old barns and farm buildings, the walling was often laid dry, without any mortar, a method that is still adhered to in field walls and farm buildings.

These dry stone walls are models of ingenious construction, for incredible as it may seem, it is almost impossible to pull out the smallest stone of a well-built wall, the stones being so admirably fitted and dovetailed together. Numerous illustrations are shown of these walls in the plates, those at Bibury and Arlington being particularly noticeable (Plates xxiii and xxiv).

The wall surface, when not left with the quarry face, and the ashlar work for the quoins and dressings, being usually coarsely cut with the chisel, no attempt being made to rub or smooth it. It is to this as much as to anything else that the walls of these buildings owe so much of their charm, for one feels that these old masons, who worked the stone, thoroughly understood their material, and, unconsciously perhaps, obtained the best value out of it in every way.

The ground floor, when there were no cellars underneath, was made of large slabs of stone, laid directly on the earth, with the result that the moisture readily soaked through, doubtless causing the rooms to be wet and unhealthy, and as damp courses were unknown when these houses were built the lower part of the walls in winter time was moist and damp. This method of laying the floors was but a slight advance on that of some century earlier, when the natural earth well trampled upon formed the only flooring. In winter, dry rushes and in summer sweet-

scented herbs were spread, but even then
they must have been damp and dirty,
and some idea of their state may be
gathered from the fact that the doorway
of the hall at Winchester was widened
to admit of carts coming in. This was
probably the origin of the raised dais
we find in so many of the old halls, and
which were evidently to enable the head
of the house to sit with some degree of
comfort, raised above the floor, which
added to his dignity and gave him a
good view of his retainers.

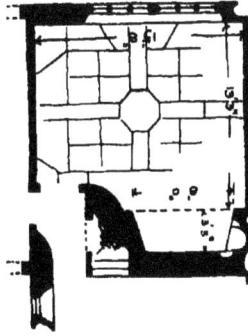

FIG. 8.   FLOOR OF COTTAGE
AT WESTON SUBEDGE.

In many cases the stones were laid to a pattern, as in the house
at Weston Subedge, (see Fig. 8), where they roughly radiate from
an octagonal centre, or as at Stanton where the paving of the hall
is made of alternate squares of blue lias and the local limestone.
In numerous cases the floors were laid according to the whim or
ingenuity of the mason. The old millstone set as a front door-
step is a very frequent sight in these Cotswold villages, as shown
in Plate xli.

The staircase always opened directly out of one or other of
the living rooms, and is generally found by the fireplace, contained in as small a place as possible, see plans, (see Figs. 1 to 8
inclusive). It was frequently circular in plan and in many of the
oldest houses was of stone, with a central newel similar to those
in church towers; another instance of the manner in which old
traditions lingered in these remote districts. Oak was the other
material used, with a series of winders round a centre post, generally cramped and awkward to get up and down.

It is noteworthy that in all these houses the staircase, even in

FIG. 9.   PORCH AT MANOR FARM, CLIFTON,
NEAR DEDDINGTON, OXON.

those of the better class, was treated solely for the purpose of utility, and was but seldom made a decorative feature, for one finds houses with rooms beautifully panelled from floor to ceiling, with fine stone chimney-pieces, yet possessing staircases with no detail worthy of notice, and in no way corresponding with the rest of the building. Some of these staircases were in semi-circular turrets projecting from the main walls, finished at the top with a conical stone slated roof. At Burford there are still a few examples left, while one very fine specimen which was at the back of the *Bear Inn* has only recently been pulled down.

Another point to be noticed is the absence of any porches, no shelter being given to the door, beyond an occasional hood, or slight projection of stone, (*see* Plates xli and xlii), and these are nearly always of later date.

In the larger houses stone porches are met with, sometimes carried up two or more storeys, and finishing in a gable, but a glance through the illustrations will show that the porches at Rissington, (Plate iii), and Mickleton, (Plate xxv), are almost isolated examples if we except those at the Manor Farms at

Ramsden, (Plate xlviii), and Clifton in Oxfordshire, (*see* Figs. 9, 10, 11), where the regular early open type is adhered to, the latter having a moulded impost at the springing of the arch.

The smaller two-roomed houses generally had but one outer door, as in the plans of those at Snowshill and Stanton, (Figs. 4 and 5), but as they grew in size and importance, two and sometimes three outer doors are not unusual, and it is only since these houses have been cut up into separate cottages that other doors and

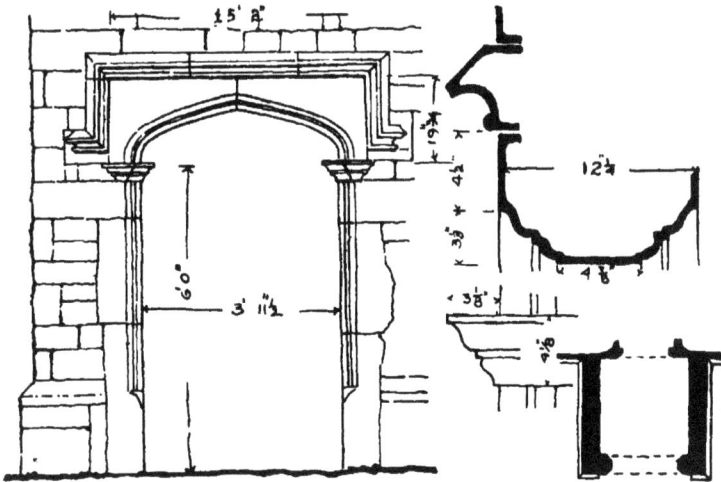

FIGS. 10, 11. PORCH AT MANOR FARM, CLIFTON.

windows have been inserted, such as were never found in the original buildings (*see* Fig. 2).

During the whole of the seventeenth century the employment of the lintol was universal, and one is struck by the almost entire absence of the arch in these buildings.

Externally the openings were never made wider than the stone would carry, and stout oak beams were used across the door and window openings inside.

The four-centred doorhead out of one stone is the commonest treatment. At first steep in outline, as at Colley Weston, (Plate xxix), Broadway and Campden (Plates xxxi, xxxii and xxxiii), and Stanway in Gloucestershire, it was later very generally flat, as in the numerous illustrations given.

The earlier doorways retained the label over the top, returning down on either side of the stone head, as in the farm-houses at Laverton and Saintbury, near Broadway, (Plates xxxv, xxxvi), and Painswick, (Plate xxxvii), or else treated with a simple cornice

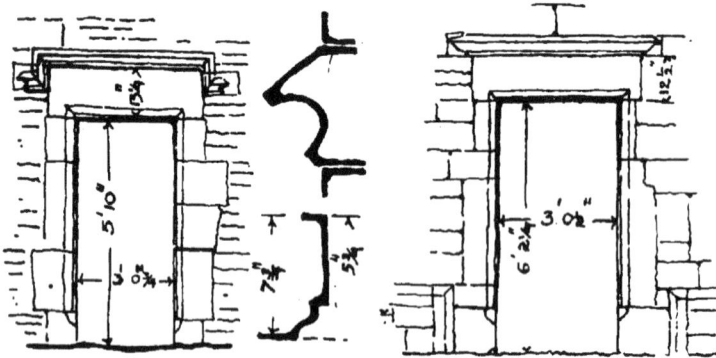

FIGS. 12, 13. DOORS AT ICCOMB, GLOS.

above the opening as at Weston Subedge and Paxford (Plates xxxviii and lxxix).

In Broadway and two or three villages adjoining, are a series of very interesting doorways, evidently executed by the same hand. The villages are only some two or three miles apart, and they were undoubtedly all carried out within a few years of each other (see Figs. 14 and 15). There is a strong Gothic feeling about the shape of the head, the carved spandrils, and the termination of the labels, but the detail of the mouldings, the late character of the carving, and the peculiarity of the stop to the jambs, all show evidence of the classical feeling that was at last pervading even these out of the way districts.

In one of the ends of the label in the village school at Aston Subedge the date 1663 is cut, and on the other the initials of the builder or owner (*see* Plate li and Fig. 14).

FIG. 14.
DOORWAY AT ASTON SUBEDGE.

FIG. 15.
DOORWAY AT BROADWAY, WORC.

Another interesting doorway is that from the Warren House at Stanton (Plate xl). Here we have a similar shaped head; moulded jambs, and the peculiar stops and rosettes in the spandrils, but instead of the label there is quite a classical treatment of architrave, frieze and cornice, all crudely detailed, but showing how, in the doorways, the builders were attempting some fresh treatment in place of the old traditional types

In some cases, as in the Northamptonshire examples, the doors had a plain straight lintol, generally treated with a fine series of mouldings, returning down the jambs, but without any label or

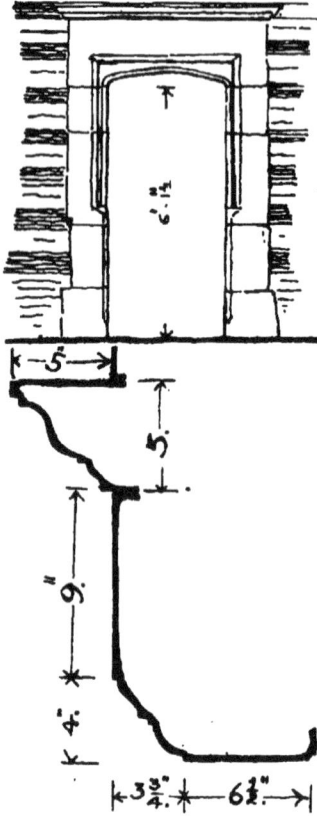

FIGS. 16, 17. DOORWAY AT GRETTON, NORTHANTS, WITH DETAILS.

FIG. 18.   A DOORWAY AT GRETTON, NORTHANTS.

cornice over, as at Gretton in Northamptonshire (*see* Fig. 18).

Occasionally the doorways were sheltered with a projecting stone hood, on moulded brackets, as at Chalford Hill near Stroud and Lechlade, (Plates xli and lx), and in Campden and Stow-on-the-Wold there is series in wood and stone of delightful and pleasing variety (*see* Figs. 19 to 21).

The doorway at Bow meadow Farm, in Laverton, (Plate xliii), is a typical Cotswold example, showing all the simple charm of the style. The deep head and large stones forming the sides all impart a sense of dignity and repose to the opening, which sets off to advantage the plain oak door.

FIG. 19. DOORHEAD AT CAMPDEN.

A pleasant variation of the flat four-centred head was obtained by inserting a key and impost stones, sometimes plain as at Bourton-on-the-Water, (*see* Fig. 19), and occasionally with the latter moulded as at Deddington.

FIG. 20. DOORHEAD AT STOW-ON-THE-WOLD.

The doorway has always been the centre of attraction and that upon which the best workmanship is most often found, for if there be

FIG. 21. DOORHEAD AT CAMPDEN.

no ornament anywhere else, it is generally here that some effort was made in that direction, as we have seen in the examples referred to.

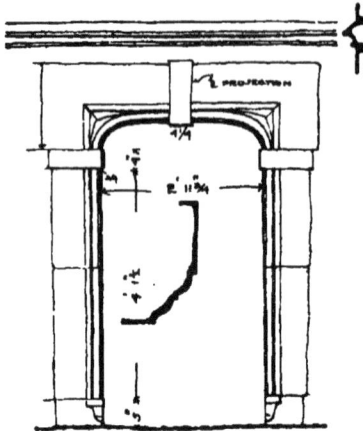

FIG. 22.   DOOR AT BOURTON-ON-THE-WATER.

It must be noted that it was in doorways, fireplaces, and the memorial tombs in the churches, that the classical influence first appeared, for it was on these features that the builders generally tried to exercise their ingenuity.

The proportion of the doorway greatly affected its decoration; a wide and low opening conveying a sense of homeliness and comfort that is seldom obtained by a tall and narrow one. And in these stone houses it was the key or focus upon which their energies were concentrated, and care and thought expended (*see* Fig. 23.)

It was in the details and furnishing of their doorways, especially the external ones, that these old Cotswold builders so excelled, for the wrought iron work, the latches

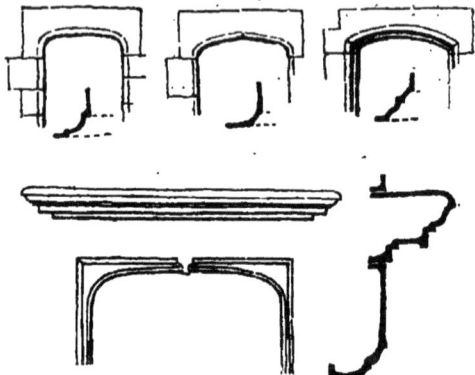

FIG. 23.   DOORHEADS AT CHIPPING CAMPDEN

and hinges, made and designed by the village smith, are full of
charm and character. Every touch shows the delight they took in their work, and how admirably suited it was to its place.

The construction of the doors—at first upright planks nailed to cross-pieces behind, allowed for the display of the beautiful hinges and fastenings still to be seen on some old examples.

The modern method of hanging doors with what are technically called "butts" is of course responsible for the loss of much beauty, for the old way of hook and band hinges, beautifully hammered and worked, added much to the general effect of the door —it provided a good opportunity for a fine piece of design on a plain oaken background; the iron work being delicately fashioned into minute tendrils and interlacing ornament, or simply forged into strong and sturdy bands.

The handles were often

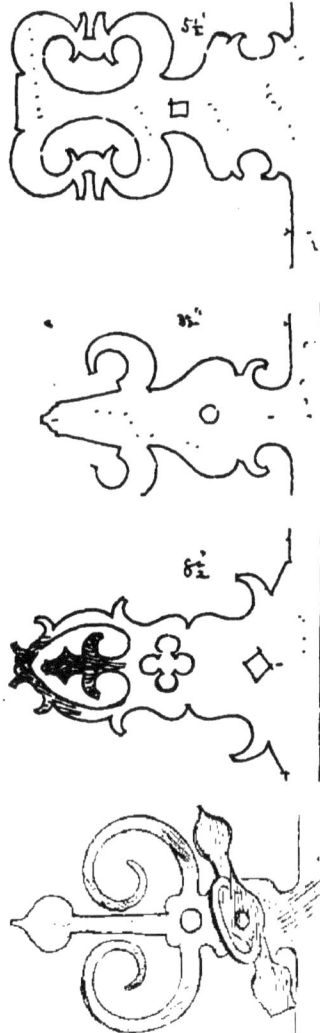

FIGS. 24, 25, 26, 27. CASEMENT FASTENINGS AND HINGES FROM BROADWAY AND OTHER PLACES.

superb pieces of craftsmanship, heavy and massively wrought, frequently serving as knocker and handle in one, surmounted on a circular or shaped plate, pierced and ornamented in all sorts of quaint designs.

The examples of doorways illustrated from Bowmeadow Farm, Laverton, (Plate xliii), and Warren House, (Plate xl), at Stanton, though plain show the hinges and fastenings found on them.

The wrought iron work to the window casements was another opportunity for the exercise of the powers of the local smith. The variety of the shaped and perforated handle-plates seems endless and hardly any are found alike. Many contained the initials of the owner of the house, ingeniously worked into the design, as in the one illustrated, from a house near Broadway, where the letter S is the initial letter of Savage, who built the house.

All this iron work, both to doors and windows, was made by the local smith, doubtless from old traditional patterns, varied and altered to suit individual tastes.

The windows are always stone mullioned, filled with lead-latticed panes and wrought-iron casements (*see* Figs. 29 and 34).

They are nearly always treated in the same way, being 12 to 16 inches wide between the mullions, and 2 to 3 feet in height, while over the head, and returning at each side, they have the hollow label or drip moulding—a survival of earlier days.

Frequently this was carried round the building as a string course above the ground floor windows, as shown in the houses illustrated from St. Paul's Street, Stamford, (Plate xliv), the alms-houses at Campden, (Plate x), and the cottages at Broadway (Plate xxvii).

Sometimes, as in the Northamptonshire examples, the label is put close above the window head, worked in the same stone,

eturning at each end as a cornice, (Plate lvii), while in Church
Street, Stroud (Plate xlv) and in Cirencester (Plate xlvi) we see
t carried almost the entire length of the building and terminated
with a drip over each end window.

The number of lights in the windows in nearly every instance

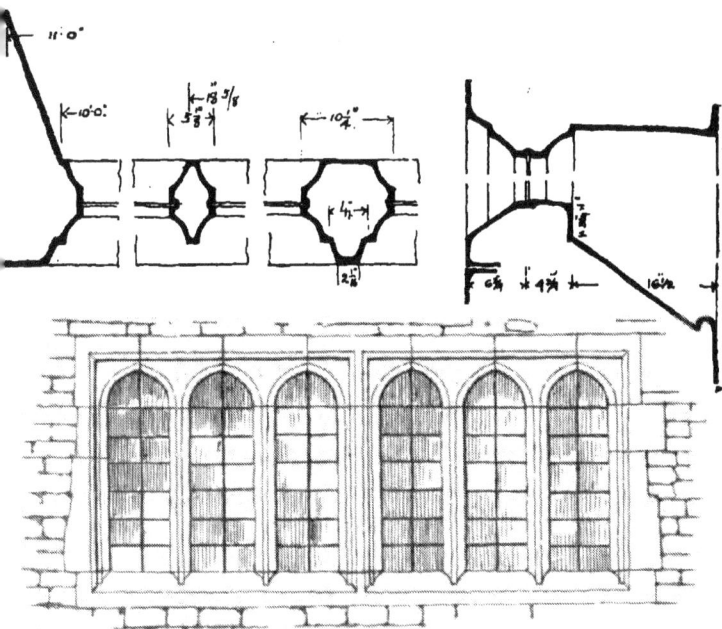

FIG. 28. WINDOW AND DETAILS, S. EDWARD'S SCHOOL, STOW-ON-THE-WOLD.

diminishes in each succeeding storey. On the ground floor the
windows have four, or sometimes six lights, with a heavier central
mullion. The next storey will have three lights, and in the gable
will be two. It was the invariable practice to lessen the number
of lights as the windows ascend into the gables, as illustrated at

Withington, Broadway, Ramsden and Weston Subedge (Plates xlvii, xlviii, and xlix).

This simple treatment allowed great elasticity of arrangement, and so long as the windows were well proportioned, and were placed in good positions for lighting the rooms, they nearly always came in well with the external elevation.

The symmetrical disposition and squareness of the plans, and the way in which they were roofed in one span, enabled the windows to be easily arranged to come centrally under a gable in every case.

In many houses dating from the beginning of the seventeenth century we find the four-centred heads, as in the Warren House at Stanton, (Plate xxxix), where this treatment is also carried into the door, and at Stow-on-the-Wold, (Plate liii), in St. Edward's School all the windows are made so (*see* Fig. 28). This shaping of the window heads is an echo of the perpendicular work of the preceding century, and in some villages it lingered for a great many years, but as a rule it was confined to the doors only, and gradually the window with the square lintols became universal.

In the picturesque early sixteenth century house at Temple Guiting, (Plates liv and lv), for many years the summer residence of the Bishops of Oxford, the windows have these shaped heads, and a few years ago they were filled with glazing containing the arms of the bishop, or a mitre, a crozier, or other ecclesiastical symbol.

The windows in every case were placed on the outer face of the wall, so that inside the deep recess gives that delightful sense of comfort that is only to be found where thick walls are used.

Bay windows are not of very frequent occurrence in the smaller houses, but in the towns and village streets they are sometimes used with very happy effect, as in the illustration of the cottages at Yarwell, (Plate lvii), and at Duddington, in Northampton-shire (Plate lviii).

The house at Yarwell is of singularly pleasant proportion, and refined detail. The entrance was on the left side of the bay, which, with the gable above, is of dressed stone, contrasting with the general walling of thin layers of rubble. The whole front is tied together by a band of stone at the cill level.

When the frontage of the street was very narrow the entrance doorway was placed in the centre, with a bay window of flat projection on either side, terminating in a gable above. A very effective instance of this is seen in the *Swan Inn* at Lechlade, shown on Plate lx, in the other shop at Colley Weston, (Plate xxix), and in the houses in St. Paul's Street, at Stamford, (Plate xliv), which unfortunately loses much of its charm through having the intermediate mullions cut out. The houses in Chipping Campden, (Plate lxi), and Callowel near Stroud, (Plate lxii), have a doorway in the centre with windows and gables placed sym-metrically on either side, giving very much the effect of the Lechlade example, without the bay treatment.

Sometimes the oriel window was used, corbeled out from the main wall, as shown in the illustration from Nassington in North-amptonshire, (Plate lxiii), and at Burford in Oxfordshire, (Fig. 83), but these can hardly be classed with the genuine Cotswold work, and are distinctly of earlier date.

Occasionally the bays are brought out square from the front of the house, as at Barford in Oxfordshire, (Plate lxiv), where the ground and first floor windows are alike in the number and treat-ment of the lights. An unusual way is the method of putting the bay in the centre of the gable, as at Lyddington in Northants, (Plate lxv), which is of three lights in width and finished with a gable at the top, but there is a sense of artificiality about the chimney stack rising from the main gable behind it that is not entirely pleasing.

No description of the windows would be complete without speaking of the dormers, the most characteristic feature of these Cotswold houses. Their origin, which is very simple, arose in the following manner. The buildings were roofed in a single span, generally com mencing about 12 or 15 feet above the ground, or some 4 feet above the bedroom floor.

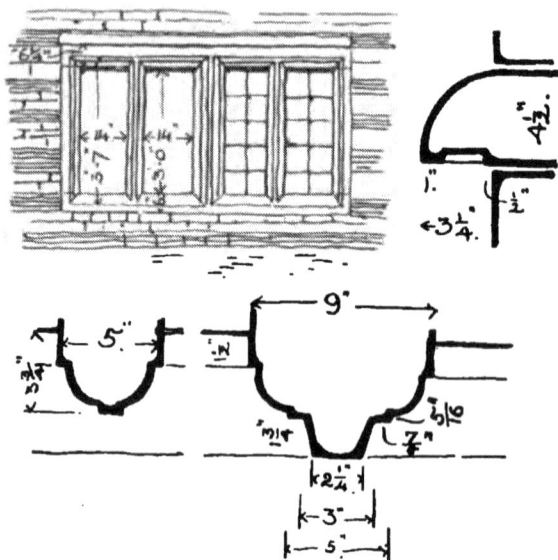

FIG. 29. WINDOW AT GRETTON, NORTHANTS.

This did not give height enough for windows to be placed under the eaves at the sides, and as the bedroom was always constructed partly in the roof, it was necessary to carry up the side walls and form a series of smaller gables, with windows in them.

These were treated in all respects similarly to the ordinary ones, finished either with a coping and finial, or else with a stone slate verge. In almost all the examples illustrated of these dormer windows are shown, but particular attention might be drawn to the charming effect of the farm-house at Willersey, Plate v, and that at Little Rissington (Plate xiii).

A later type of dormer is occasionally seen, formed entirely in the roof, as illustrated in the Dean Row, Coln St. Aldwyn (Plate lxxv), and Medford House, (Plate lxxx), but they lack the charm of the earlier ones.

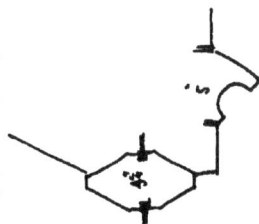

FIG. 30. TYPICAL HOLLOW "PERPENDICULAR" LABEL.

Another window also peculiar to this Cotswold district, though again of much later date, is that illustrated in the Baker's and Carpenter's Shops at Bourton-on-the-Hill, (Plates lxxvii and lxxviii), and in the cottage at Broadway (Plate lxxvi). Here we have a simple bay window with a stone base, above which is a framework of wood, and lead-lights, covered by a stone slated roof and generally accompanied by shutters, folding back against the wall on either side.

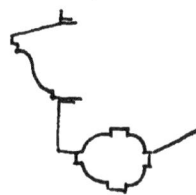

Mullions.

These windows are only found on the ground floor rooms, and are most picturesque additions to the houses they adorn.

Centre Mullion.

There was during the 17th century a great similarity in the mouldings of domestic buildings, and this was so whether the houses were large or small.

The earliest form of moulding, and one that continued in use in a modified form longer than any others, was the hollow moulded mullion and jambs (see Fig. 28).

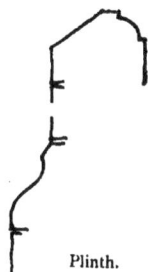

Plinth.

This usually accompanies the Tudor or Gothic-shaped head, as at Stow-on-the-Wold, (Plate liii), and was eventually superseded by the ovolo-shaped mullion, as in Fig. 29.

FIGS. 31, 32, 33. MOULDINGS FROM THE ALMSHOUSES, CAMPDEN.

D

The hollow " perpendicular " label was used indiscriminately with both these types, and lasted as long as any other features in the houses (*see* Fig. 30).

Occasionally the centre mullion—where six or four lights are used in one window, had the jamb moulding repeated as an additional fillet, (*see* Figs. 28 and 32), generally square but sometimes round as in the Almshouses at Campden, where the label moulding again varies (*see* Figs. 31–33).

FIG. 34.   WINDOW AND DETAILS AT WANSFORD, NORTHANTS.

The ordinary window detail was the plain chamfered mullion with the hollow moulding over, as shown in Fig. 30, and this was universal throughout the whole district for a great number of years, and is found even where the entire design of the house is altered, and almost every other detail changed, as at Medford House, Mickleton, (Plates lxxx to lxxxiii), where the windows are practically the only features retaining the old traditional forms.

The sizes of the stonework to the windows is invariably the

same, the mullions some 5 inches to 5¼ inches wide, with the larger central one anything between 7 inches and 9 inches, the heads about 7 inches to 8 inches in depth, the cills shallower, and the hollow label over, some 4 inches deep, returning on either side the depth of the head.   Every village mason knew and kept to these proportions, and consequently repeated them time after time.

With the gradual change in style towards the end of the seventeenth century and the introduction of classic detail, the lights became wider and higher, and as the rooms too became loftier, transomes and upper lights were inserted, as will be seen in the example on Plate ix.

In Burford there is a very charming house, dated 1672, facing the main street, which contains some extremely pleasing detail of this transitional period, where the mullion style still prevailed, but evidencing the endeavour to graft the newer fashion on the older forms.

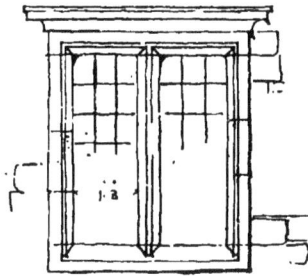

FIG. 35.   WINDOW AT ICCOMB.

At Colley Weston in Northants is another variety, where the mullions are still ovolo moulded, but with a hollow treated as an architrave all round, dying out on to a projecting splayed cill, and covered by a cornice over the head.

The example from Iccomb in Gloucestershire, (Fig. 35), is plainer; here the chamfered mullion and jambs are used, but all round a raised fillet forms an architrave from which a hollow moulded cornice springs.

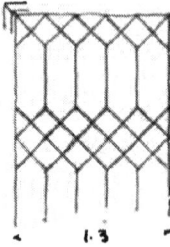

FIG. 36. LEAD-
GLAZING FROM
BROADWAY.

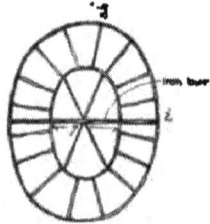

FIG. 38. AN OVAL WINDOW
FROM MICKLETON.

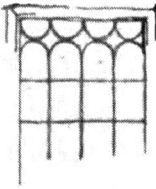

FIG. 37. LEAD-
GLAZING FROM
TEWKESBURY.

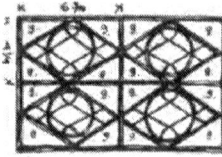

9. DENOTES GLAZING
THE OTHER PARTS ARE
UNGLAZED.

FIG. 39. LEADED VENTILA-
TOR FROM A HOUSE
NEAR CAMPDEN.

The lead latticed glazing of these houses forms quite an integral part of their construction, and a stone-mullioned window without its accompanying small panes of glass is but a sorry sight.

In the earlier houses we find the diamond panes, or patterns based upon a variation of the diamond and square, sometimes very small and intricate, as in Fig. 36 from Broadway, but always such as the village glazier could cut and put together. Any attempts at circular or interlacing leading are only occasionally met with, as at Winchcombe and Tewkesbury, (Fig. 37), where the tops of the lights are rounded, giving a little variation to the monotony of the square panes.

Towards the middle of the seventeenth century the rectangular oblong panes became very popular, and continued so down to the close of the eighteenth with but little change; indeed it is doubtful if any form of latticed lights were so suitable with either stone or wooden mullioned windows.

The oval windows in the gables were occasionally filled with patterned leading as at Mickleton, (Fig. 38), and sometimes in dairies and such places the lead was left unglazed for ventilation—a quaint example being given from a house near Campden (Fig. 39).

Here, as in everything else in the district, the ingenuity and spontaneous originality of the craftsman is very marked. This was doubtless a pattern worked out by himself, and though it does not pretend to anything in the way of design, yet the forms selected are suitable and it serves its purpose admirably, besides giving a pleasant touch of character to the window it fills.

The colour of the old glass again is noticeable, varying from pale amber to bottle green; somewhat unsuitable for seeing through, as it distorts the vista outside in a painful manner, but yet seeming to adapt itself to the old stone windows in a way that quite clear glass perhaps would not do.

The leading of the small panes of glass always enabled the texture of the masonry walls to be carried, as it were, through the windows without a break, getting a continuity of surface that is very pleasing, and which these old builders thoroughly appreciated.

The mistake so many people make to-day is in glazing the windows, with single sheets of glass, producing a cold effect inside and breaking up the exterior with cavernous spots of black, and emphasizing the mullions in a manner that was never intended.

It would of course be wearisome and profitless to go through the category of trifling variations of the detail of doors and windows, as they differed but little from those in general use all over the country, and where they did the changes were evidently attributable to the whim and ingenuity of the mason, who wanted to be in the fashion and adopt the newer styles, and who having probably once seen them in other parts of the country, interpreted them in his own work as best he could.

In dealing with the subject of windows, the panel decorations placed over them in the gables must not be overlooked.

These, like most other features in the houses, were distinctly local in their treatment, consisting in many instances of merely a small single light, either filled with glass or made solid.

In Northamptonshire, as a glance at the illustrations will show, they were nearly always either square or diamond-shaped panels containing a date and initials, as at the *White Lion* at Oundle (Plate xciii), St. Paul's Street, Stamford, shown in Figs. 40 and 41, or else projecting with a moulded cornice above, as at Colley Weston, (Plate xxix), and occasionally taking the form of a ton (Plate lxvii).

FIG. 40. A GABLE IN S. PAUL'S STREET, STAMFORD.

In the neighbourhood of Broadway, the oval or circular form was universal, the opening bordered with a series of small rustications. This treatment was evidently popular and lasted for many years, as the examples at Paxford, (Plate lxx), Willersey, (Plate lxxxiv), and Stanton, (Plate iv), show, and it appears again on either side of the central window in the front of Medford House at Mickleton, (Plate lxxx), a very charming composition, many years later in date than the other examples.

These openings were doubtless originally glazed, as in the case of the small opening at Top Farm, Broadway,.(*see* Fig. 42), and in the house just referred to, but often they are found plastered up on the outside. Sometimes, as at Weston Subedge, the panel took the form of a plain sinking with a curved head, (Plate xxxviii), and the form of two lancet lights cut out of a single stone, as at Stanton, (*see* Fig. 43), is not uncommon.

FIG. 41. PANEL FROM THE GABLE AT STAMFORD HILL.

At first sight this looks like some early thirteenth century work inserted in the more modern building, but a closer inspection reveals the handiwork of the seventeenth century village craftsman.

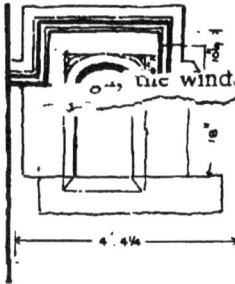

FIG. 42. GABLE OPENING, TOP FARM, BROADWAY.

In the Stroud district a favourite form was the round cut out of one piece of square stone, as at the *Plough* at Callowel (Plate lxii), and in many of the larger houses designs of more pretentious character are often seen.

Square stones, built in flush with the walling, and bearing a date and initials, either sunk or raised, were very popular, and were generally placed over the doorway and sometimes worked in the actual lintol itself.

These tablets, generally of the seventeenth and eighteenth centuries, in some form or other, either enriched or plain, are found more or less all through these districts following the belt of limestone,

FIG. 43. AT STANTON.

that traverses England diagonally from the Dorsetshire to the Yorkshire coasts (*see* Figs. 44 to 49).

Where brick or wood are the ordinary building materials, it is seldom that such tablets are seen, but stone offered a ready material

FIG. 44.
AT GRETTON,
NORTHANTS.

FIG. 45.
AT SPRATTON,
NORTHANTS.

FIG. 46.   AT
EAST HADDON,
NORTHANTS.

at hand for the easy exercise of local fancy, and much quaint ingenuity was displayed in the fashioning of them.

They are doubtless a lingering survival of the old custom of

FIG. 47.   AT THE
MANOR HOUSE,
GRETTON.

FIG. 48.   AT
CHIPPING CAMPDEN.

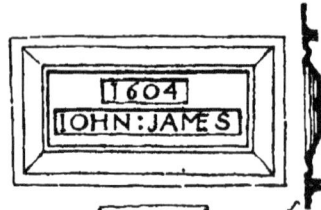

FIG. 49.
AT STANTON.

placing the owner's coat of arms over the entrance door, and are interesting if only for that reason.

The simplest form is just a slab of stone, with the initials and

date upon it, within a panel, the disposition of the initials generally following one fashion—that of the surname at the top—
the Christian names of the man and his wife beneath, and the date
at the bottom.

These stones are very frequently seen upon the houses in
Gloucestershire and Northants, sometimes two and even more
being on the same house, showing the changes of occupation they
have undergone at different periods (*see* Fig. 49).

It seems a pity that so simple a means of adding some small
amount of interest and individuality to the entrance of a house
should be but seldom seen now-a-days, but like most other local
customs this is rapidly dying out.

In the smaller houses, as the rooms were usually about 7 or
8 feet high, the windows were always one light in height, and it
was only towards the end of the century, and in the larger buildings, that a transome and upper light became common.

It is the lowness of the storeys, and the length of the windows,
that give the charming sense of good proportion common to
nearly all these small houses and cottages, for though the old
builders may have had but rudimentary ideas upon the soundness
of building, they have never been excelled as regards the beautiful and simple proportions of their houses.

Although they were all built on traditional lines and well-
recognized principles, yet we may traverse the district from end
to end and not find two houses exactly alike.

The style was elastic, and the arrangement of the roofs enabled the builders to dispose of the windows and gables as they
pleased. It is this infinite diversity of form and variety of
treatment that make these stone-built houses stand out so pre-
eminently as a phase of domestic architecture, quite apart from
anything else in the country.

If we turn to the plan of the house at Aston Subedge, (*see* Fig. 50), we find it consists of one simple parallelogram. The main doorway, (*see* Fig. 51), is in the centre, with a room immediately right and left of it, and through the latter a smaller one, the back kitchen or brew-house.

The original staircase was by the chimney, which contains two wide fireplaces.

As the ground falls from right to left a series of steps lead out of the porch into the smaller living room, which has an additional outer doorway.

This house is now used as the village school, and its interior

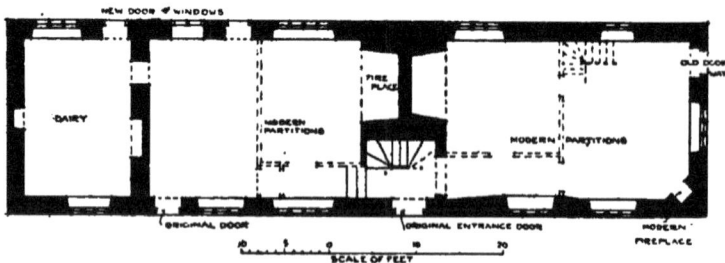

FIG. 50. PLAN OF HOUSE AT ASTON SUBEDGE (NOW THE VILLAGE SCHOOL).

has been considerably altered by partitions, but the simplicity of the original plan is reflected in the elevation, which shows a roof unbroken from end to end, with the exception of two small gables over the entrance doorway, and the window beside it.

The farmhouse at Willersey, (Plate v), has a somewhat similar plan with a series of windows carried up as dormers into the roof above, all thoroughly well balanced and giving on the exterior a clue to the arrangement of the rooms within. The heights and widths of the windows, and the disposal of the gables, leave nothing to be desired. The whole composition, free from any striving after effect, is an example of simple direct building and a lesson in the sensible use of material.

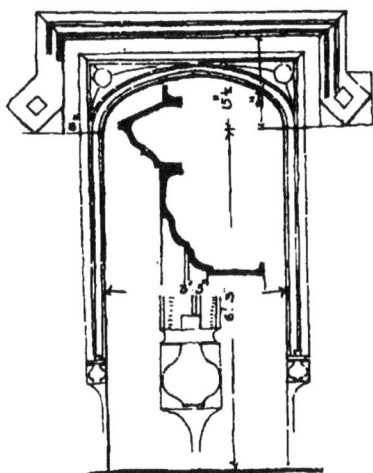

FIG. 51. DOORWAY OF THE VILLAGE SCHOOL, ASTON SUBEDGE.

The chimneys are amongst the most characteristic features of these Cotswold houses, and are invariably carried up, massive and solid, and suggest wide ingle nooks and cosy firesides, as in the instance shown from Medford House at Mickleton, (Plate lxxxiii), where the stack is taken up the full width and is finished with a roof having the chimney in the centre of the gable.

The stacks at Snowshill, (Plate xxvi), the Warren House at Stanton, (Plate xxxix), the cottages at Ebrington, (Plate lxxxv), at Humphries Farm, near Stroud, (Plate lxxxvi), and Woodchester (Plate lxxxvii), are typical of the external treatment of the fireplaces.

They were always placed centrally over the ridge or on the apex of the gables at either end, and when the stacks were at the sides of the building, then on smaller roofs connecting them with the main one,

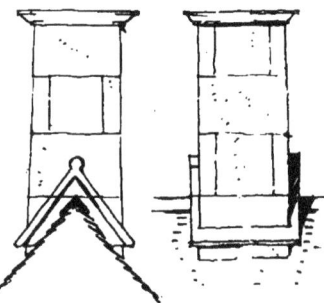

FIG. 52.   STACKS AT BROADWAY.

as in the house at Weston Subedge (Plate xxxviii).

The chimney-stack immediately above the roof, and up to the base moulding, was invariably square, while on the other side, and coinciding with the gable coping, is a projecting weather course, under which the slates were tucked, and which also returned along the bottom edge (*see* Fig. 52). This treatment, which is invariable with the stone roofs, can be seen in numerous houses, and is shown at Weston Subedge, (Plate xxxviii), at Temple Guiting, (Plates liv and lv), and Broadway (Plate xxxi).

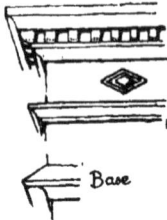

When the roof is cleared, the flues are often built separately, either square or diagonally, in clusters of three or four, always made of slabs of sawn and dressed stone, about three or four inches thick, and eight or ten inches in depth, standing on edge and breaking joint over each other, tied together at the top by a moulded stone cap of simple section, as at Withington, (Plate xlvii), and Broadway (Plate xxxi).

Sometimes this cap was treated as a cornice with architrave and frieze, enriched with sunk patterns, raised diamonds, or other devices that took the mason's fancy, as in the house at Broadway, (*see* Fig. 53), and at Campden (Plate xxxii). Fig. 56 gives some characteristic sections of these cornice-

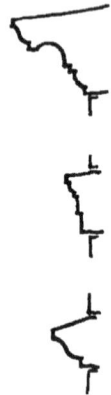

FIG. 53.   CAP OF A
BROADWAY CHIMNEY.

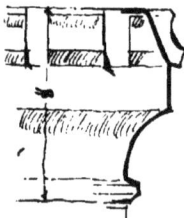

FIG. 54.
AT STANTON.

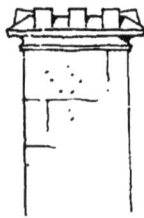

FIG. 55.
AT BURFORD.

FIG. 56.
TYPICAL
PROFILES
OF
CHIMNEY
CORNICES.

cappings. Occasionally the earlier Gothic treatment is seen, where we find the battlemented top as at Stanton and Burford, (Figs. 54 and 55), but these are somewhat isolated instances and only emphasize, by their rarity, the frequency with which the others were used.

Many of the earlier chimneys still remain in this part of the country, some incorporated in work of a later date.

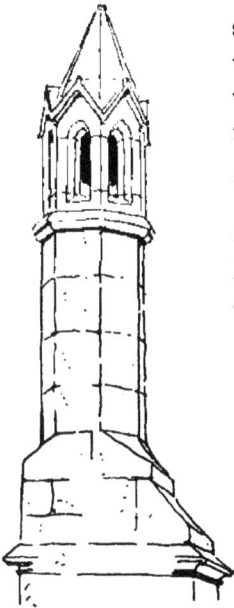

FIG. 57.
CHIMNEY FROM KINGHAM.

These generally consist of octagonal or circular shafts pierced with lancet openings, crowned at the top with a pyramidal roof, as in those illustrated from Kingham, Bredon, and Bibury (Figs. 57, 58, and 59).

In the arrangements of the roofs too the old Cotswold builders greatly excelled, and here we find the most characteristic features of their buildings.

If we analyse them in order to discover what constitutes their charm, we find that they resolve themselves into very simple forms, but the masterly way in which, in almost every instance, the grouping and disposal of the gables, dormers, and chimney-stacks was managed is worthy of admiration.

FIG. 58. CHIMNEY ON A
BARN AT BREDON, WORC.

FIG. 59. CHIMNEY
FROM BIBURY.

The roofs were nearly always treated in the same way, having a fairly steep pitch, of about 55 degrees, and being hung with stone slates, graduated in thickness from the eaves to the ridge, where the thinnest and smallest are placed, and crowned on the top with a stone cresting of some simple section.

Here we see the effect of material upon design and construction, and how these old country builders realized that one was dependent on the other.

The nature of the stone of which the slates, or "slats," as they are locally called, were made, limits them to certain sizes, so that the stone roofs of somewhat low pitch, with the large and heavy slates found in Sussex and the North of England, are quite unknown here.

As soon as the angle of the roof was flattened the slates had to be larger, for the small slates would not keep the wet out, and so after finding the exact pitch at which they had least strain on the pins and were most weather proof, the old slates never varied it.

The names of the slates are exceedingly quaint, and doubtless have their origin in very remote times, but the slaters are chary of using them before strangers, and it is only amongst themselves that one hears them spoken. The bottom or under slates at the eaves—the one bedded on the top of the walls—is called a "cussome." This has a slight tilt downwards, to throw the water off, and projects some seven or eight inches. Above this the eaves commence with long and short "eighteens" down to long and short "elevens"; then we have long and short "wivetts," "becks," "bachelors," "movedays," "cuttings," and long and short "cocks" at the apex under the cresting.

They are hung dry with oak or deal pegs, which are driven tight into holes in the slates, whilst they are being sorted to sizes, or else nailed in the ordinary manner. When plastered or torched with hair mortar, level with the underside of the laths, they will last for years, as so many existing buildings testify.

The "valleys" are formed of the same slates, in a wide sweep with no hard line of demarcation where the roofs intersect, laid in regular formation and ranging with the ordinary slating.

Each valley slate has its distinctive name, the centre one being the " bottomer," with two " lie-byes " on either side, and above and below in the next courses two " skews " to break joint. Numerous examples of this work in the roofs, are shown in the plates, as for instance Nos. 27 and 94.

There are of course only certain districts where the stone from which these slates are made is found. It has to easily laminate in thin beds, to be hard and weather resisting, and without sand-holes or flaws.

In Northamptonshire there is a bed of stone, at Colley Weston and Easton, which laminates very freely, and has formed from a very early period the prevalent roofing material of the locality. These Northamptonshire slates, as a rule, are of a larger size than the Oxford and Gloucestershire ones, obtained at the celebrated Stonesfield and Guiting and Eyford Quarries, but all are equally durable and weather resisting.

The method of getting the slates is interesting, as it differs from the general custom of splitting by hand.

In October a piece of ground at the quarry is measured off and the upper eight or ten feet of loose " brash " is cleared away, this process being called " ridding." The " pendal," as the stone for the slates is called, is then uncovered and wheeled to the top of the ground, laid down flat, and roughly fitted together as nearly as it will allow, in thicknesses varying from two to twelve or fourteen inches, just as it comes from the quarry.

It has then to lie and wait for the winter frosts, which swell the beds of natural moisture in the " pendal," and when a thaw sets in, a few blows of the hammer soon separate the layers, which are then cut to the sizes required and sorted ready for use. But should the winters be mild, the stone has to wait until the following year.

The ridge cresting or " crease," as it is locally called, was sawn out of a block of stone in a very simple and economical way. A piece of stone nine inches or ten inches wide and about two or three feet long is stood on edge, and a series of saw cuts in the form of a V made in it from end to end, the pieces are then lifted out, the top sharp arris and bottom edges squared off, and the ridge is ready for use. By this means a comparatively small piece of stone will make sufficient cresting to cover a very large quantity of roofing. (Figs. 60 and 61 show this method.)

Owing possibly to the cost or difficulty of procuring lead in these country towns and villages, the builders did without it, and the houses, as mentioned before, however large or small, were always planned so that they could be roofed in one single span.

FIGS. 60, 61. METHOD OF FORMING RIDGE CRESTING.

Hips, or any cutting or mitreing of the slates was absolutely unknown in a genuine stone-roofed house, and there are invariably gables with the slates carried out over them to form a verge, or butting, up to and tucked under the stone coping. Even at the junction of a lower roof with a higher one, where the ridge dies in, no lead was used, but a length of cresting was turned upside down to throw the water off, as shown in the inn at Willersey, (Plate lxxxiv), or the cottage at Bourton-on-the-Hill (Plate lxxviii).

The old craftsmen could do almost anything with these stone slates. The clever way in which the outside ovens are roofed, with the slates worked up on the curve as at Snowshill, (Plate xxvi), or over the circular outer staircases with pointed roofs, and again in the beautiful dovecots, of which so many still remain scattered about the country side is truly remarkable. A good example of these is still standing at Bibury; it is circular, with a later cupola addition on the top (*see* Fig. 62). Another at Southrop shows the traditional gabled treatment with four equal sides.

In this latter instance we see how successfully the roofs were treated, for a simple square on plan, roofed as this is, produces a building full of charm, and gives effects of light and shade that perhaps no other form of roof could.

FIG. 62.   DOVECOTE AT BIBURY.

It is interesting to note here a wall at Stow-on-the-Wold in which the pigeon holes have been built at regular intervals, as shown in Fig. 63.

Then again the way in which difficulties were got over is always instructive.

E

In many buildings we find the stone bays, with canted sides carried up to the eaves without any awkward problems to solve, but as soon as the roof was reached it meant either a lead flat and parapet, or else some way of getting back into a flat gable, and many and ingenious were the means adopted to attain this.

Sometimes it was clumsily managed, but at Lechlade is seen the simplest possible way, (Plate lx), while in other cases, as in the Northamptonshire examples, the junctions between the canted sides of the bay and the gable over, were made a specially delightful feature, as shown in Fig. 40. But however it was treated the full gable overhanging the sides is never quite satisfactory, always having a certain sense of weakness and makeshift, never seen in the gable over the square bay.

For stone houses there is no more beautiful or suitable material than these slates as a roof covering, which harmonize so admirably, and seem almost to grow from the walls supporting them. When old and covered with lichens their colour is indescribably exquisite, and seen in their proper setting amidst trees and fields the general tone of silver grey harmonizes admirably with the surrounding landscape. Even when new they are pleasing, as the slates are of all shades of greys, browns, and yellows.

Unfortunately, owing to the advent of railways and cheap means of locomotion, the purple blue Welsh slates, and even

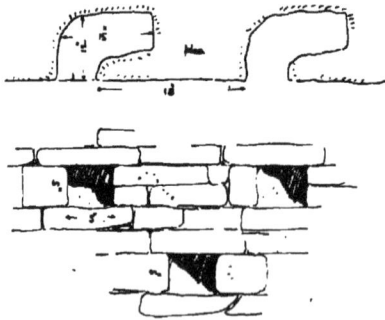

FIG. 63.   PIGEON HOLES IN THE WALL,
STOW-ON-THE-WOLD.

galvanised iron, are now becoming common. Both materials are
doubtless good in themselves, but they are out of all harmony
with the buildings, and do not in any way blend with them.

Such " foreign " materials possibly have the advantage of
being cheaper and easier to carry, the stone slates requiring slightly
heavier timbering, more care and trouble in fixing, and occasional
repairing. But these are poor reasons to set against the fact that
houses and barns two hundred and more years old still stand
covered with their original roofs.

The slates, if properly seasoned at first, are almost imperish-
able, for no frost or wet will touch them ; they can be taken off
and re-hung again and again, and as a consequence old ones com-
mand a ready sale and are eagerly sought for.

It seems unreasonable to go miles afield to obtain an inferior,
if cheaper, material, when the better one lies literally at one's
feet, but this now happens, and as a result it becomes more and
more difficult to get slaters who understand the work, as the
craft, like that of the thatcher, seems to be dying out for lack of
employment.

Many of the modern stone slates are not so good as the old,
not by reason of any failing in the quality of the stone, but simply
from the demand for mechanical precision which seems to pervade
all trades to-day.

They are now made as smooth and thin as possible, and with
all the edges dressed square and true, and when hung look hard
and cold and but little different, except in colour, from a blue
slate roof; possessing none of the softness and texture of the old
roofs. Nor are they so durable, the old slates being rough and
uneven, never laid close, and the wet and moisture soon dried
out of them ; but the new ones, closely fitted and bedded tight
down, one on the other, the circulation of air between them is

prevented and the wet retained much longer, giving a better chance to frost.

In a great degree this is due to the irregularity of the old

FIG. 64. FINIAL AT WESTON SUBEDGE.

FIG. 65. FINIAL OF GABLE AT TOP FARM, BROADWAY.

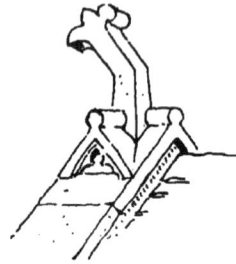

FIG. 66. GOTHIC FINIAL ON A BARN AT LONGBOROUGH.

FIG. 67. AT CAMPDEN.

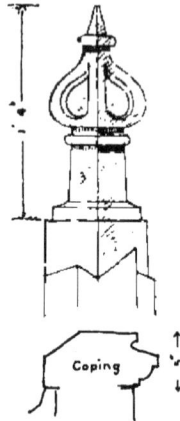

FIG. 68. FINIAL FROM CHASTLETON.

FIG. 69. FROM BROADWAY.

slates, which gives such a texture to the surface of the roofs and which one so sadly misses in many new ones. The old slates were always thick and rough, with irregularities of surface and uneven edges, and the old oak riven laths, on which the slates were hung, not being always straight, the bottom edges varied and did not carry a hard straight line, thus giving a charmingly diversified effect.

In connection with the roofs the variety of the gable termi-

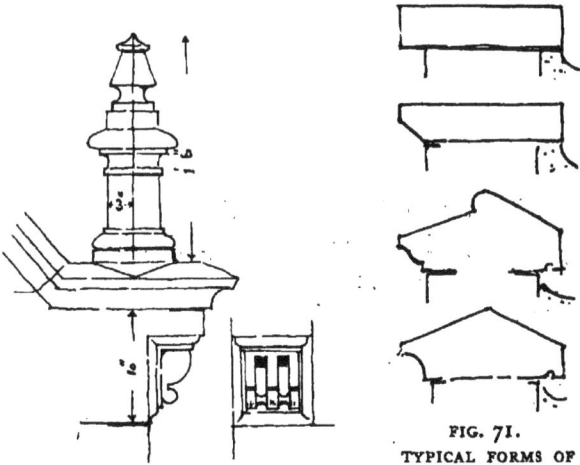

FIG. 70. FROM BROADWAY.

FIG. 71.
TYPICAL FORMS OF
GABLE COPINGS.

nations is very worthy of notice, for perhaps in no district of England is such diversity of form and detail found.

They are generally placed on the apex of the gables, but sometimes on the springers as well, and many are pierced and cut in a delightful manner (see, inter alia, Figs. 64, 65 and 70). They are found all through the stone districts, but in the neighbourhood of Campden, the villages round, and in parts of Northants, there are some extremely pleasing examples.

These finials express as much as anything else the individuality

of the men who made them.   In every village and town, as before
mentioned, the style of building and proportions were almost
traditional, and there was little or no departure from it, but these

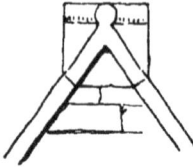

FIG. 72.   GABLE TERMINATION FROM
SNOWSHILL.

FIG. 73. GABLE TERMINATION
FROM WINCHCOMBE.

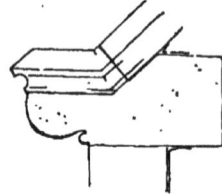

finials were little instances of personal detail that the country
mason let himself go upon, and some are much stronger and more
full of vitality than others—notice the excellent open ones at
Weston Subedge, (Fig. 64), and Willersey, (Fig. 68), and Top Farm
Broadway, (Figs. 65, 69, 70), and the early Gothic example on the
tithe barn at Longborough (Fig. 66).

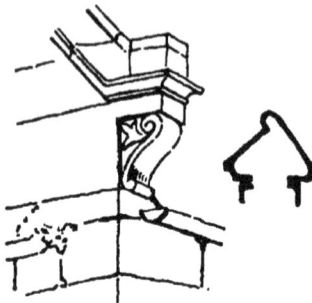

FIG. 74.   KNEELER FROM
DEDDINGTON, OXON.

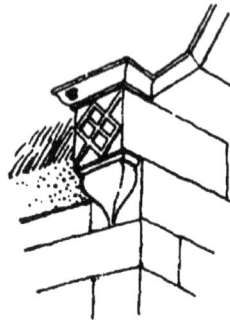

FIG. 75.   KNEELER FROM
CRETTON, NORTHANTS.

The gable copings also are of simple outline ; those to the
more unpretentious cottages being no more than a flat stone projecting slightly, back and front, with the slates tucked closely

under behind—others again have a more Gothic outline. We find many and various ways of treating the springing apex generally quite plain—sometimes as at Snowshill, (Fig. 72), and sometimes as at Deddington, (Fig. 74), and Gretton, (Fig. 75), and Broadway (Fig. 76).

The examples shown in many of the Northamptonshire houses are quite unique, and are rather different from the Cotswold ones.

A very frequent and favourite treatment is to reverse the apex with a small cusped opening under, and kept quite plain, (*see* Fig. 75), an echo of earlier perpendicular tradition. Sometimes this was on the actual ridge cresting itself, when no stone coping was used, as at Callowel Farm (Plate xciv).

In many of the houses all through the Cotswolds there are small features of this kind, emphasizing the thoughtful way in which the builders settled the problems they had to deal with.

Of timber-built houses, we do not find in the hill country any large amount, but directly we get off the stone and into the valleys, where oak was grown, we find half timber and plaster

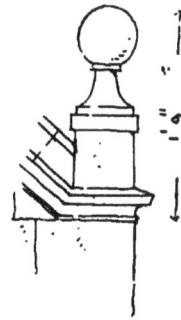

FIG. 76.
AT BROADWELL.

houses, and these combined with the stonework make most picturesque buildings.

Under the slopes of the Bredon Hills there are whole villages in which this treatment is adopted, and it is found in the Stroud valley, as at Leonard Stanley, (Plate c), and again in the Warwickshire vale. All these places are bordering on the stone districts, and in all a mixture of the two materials is met with.

Plaster or rough cast houses are somewhat plentiful, though it is questionable whether this rough cast—which is generally of eighteenth century date—was not, on the stone houses at any rate, used as a protection against the driving rain, which in this part of the country penetrates even these thick stone walls.

In the houses at Burford, (Plates xcvi and xcvii), it is doubtless put on over the timber framing below, and at Woodchester, (Plate lxxxvii), a stone-built house is so treated.

At Winchcombe, Stow-on-the-Wold, Cirencester, etc., there are numerous instances of this kind of work, in which imitation quoins are stamped at the angles and around the windows.

A very fine house at Stow-on-the-Wold, now unfortunately pulled down, had the front covered with geometrical patterns in plaster, with raised mouldings, diapers and patterns of a type not found in other districts and possessing a distinct individuality (see Fig. 77).

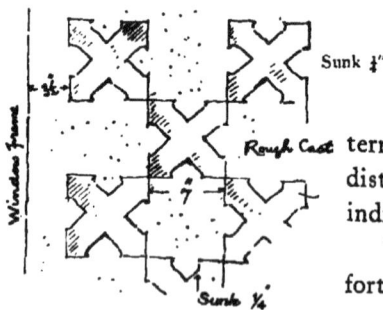

FIG. 77. PLASTER PATTERNS FORMERLY ON A HOUSE AT STOW-ON-THE-WOLD.

The bulk of this work is unfortunately only executed in a material that will not withstand the weather, and sad havoc is being wrought with much of what still remains.

In the smaller houses and cottages, though the general fabric was precisely similar to the manor houses, and the detail of doors and windows, chimneys and roofs was the same, the treatment of the interior was much simplified, and but little ornament or decoration is met with.

Instead of richly-panelled walls and delicately-fashioned plaster ceilings, we find plastered walls and roughly-hewn joists of oak or elm, with only occasionally a moulded beam.

Occasionally there are plaster ceilings, panelled rooms, and decorated fireplaces, but though these have suffered from rough usage and neglect, yet the workmanship of everything, however plain or simple, inside these houses was always the same, thoroughly honest and good.

It seemed to be a maxim that every house, irrespective of its

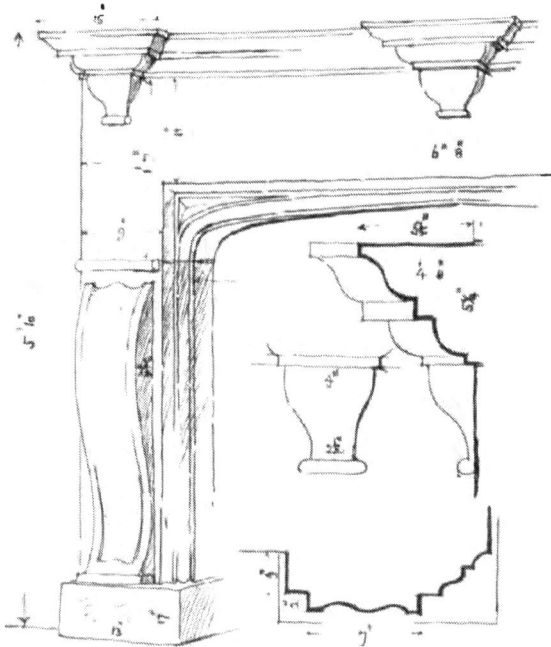

FIG. 78. STONE CHIMNEYPIECE, MANOR HOUSE, TURKDEAN, DATED 1588.

size, should be of the best workmanship and contain some work of interest and charm.

It must be remembered, however, that most of the larger houses were not in the first instance built as farmhouses and cottages, but having fallen on evil days, they have arrived at their present condition and occupation.

In the great houses, after the shell was built, it often happened that strange workmen were imported to execute the internal finishings, but in the simple buildings, where the work was plain it was all done by local workmen and with native home-grown material, and always has a dignity and simple charm that is very pleasing.

As we noticed before, it was on the fireplace and its surroundings that any little display of architectural design was generally lavished, and in some of the houses quite decorative treatments were adopted. The fireplace and chimneypiece at Turkdean, (*see* Fig. 78), is an instance of a somewhat unusual character, whilst that at Darlingscott, shown in Fig. 79, is of the commoner type.

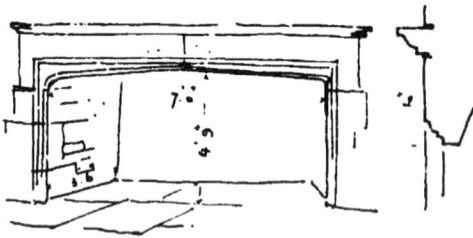

FIG. 79.   FIREPLACE AT DARLINGSCOTT.

Wood was the universal fuel, so that fires were always on the hearth, and hence we find hardly any wrought iron work, with the exception of the fireplace where the cooking was done.

There is a good deal of characteristic building of late date, and many of the houses and cottages have been added to in Queen Anne's reign.

One typical example of a building of this date is Medford House, near Campden, (Plates lxxx to lxxxiii), of which the plan is given in Fig. 80.

Here a more symmetrical arrangement has been adopted, the

entrance being placed in the centre, with slightly projecting wings on either side.

The windows are the usual stone mullioned ones, traditional in detail, but the pedimented doorway, dentilled cornice and hipped roofs all show the classical influence of the times.

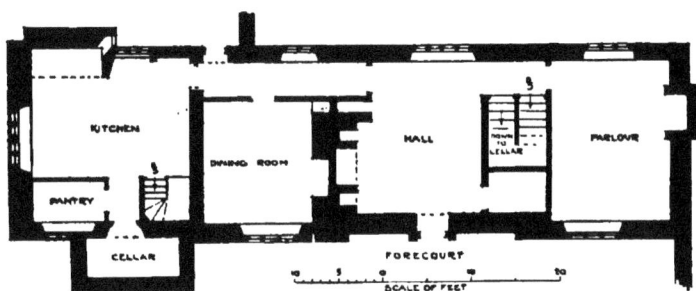

FIG. 80. PLAN OF MEDFORD HOUSE, MICKLETON.

The squareness of the entrance court, flanked by piers with well-designed urns, (see Fig. 81), is quite a departure from the haphazard though picturesque approaches to the ordinary houses.

Painswick and the Stroud valley contain many remarkably fine specimens of Queen Anne and Early Georgian work,—indeed it is freely scattered throughout all the towns and villages, but such work hardly falls within the scope of these notes, and merits a study by itself.

The ancient town of Burford is situated on the borders of Oxfordshire, and like many villages in the Cotswolds, lies in one of the narrow valleys that intersect the hills in all directions.

The surrounding country is typical of the whole district, with its wide stretches of bare uplands, dotted with groups of beech and elm trees and grey homesteads. The old town is similar to many others, with its broad and open High Street, scrupulously clean, and bordered by quaint houses of all ages and styles.

Fifty years ago it was a thriving and prosperous place, but the advent of railways has long since left it high and dry and out of the world of to-day. It was once renowned for the manufacture of paper, malt, sail cloth, saddlery and bell-casting. But though it has lost all its trade, and activity and bustle, yet Burford of to-day is a peaceful spot to visit. Like all these towns, it once played its part in history, and during the Civil Wars King Charles I was several times there. Queen Elizabeth hunted in Wychwood forest, and William III spent his birthday there in 1695 on his way to Oxford.

FIG. 81.   ENTRANCE PIER AT MEDFORD
HOUSE, MICKLETON.

Burford is well known for its Manor House, built about the year 1600 by Sir Lawrence Tanfield, whose monument is now in the church. The history of the house is indeed the history of Burford, but can hardly be considered as belonging to the class of smaller houses.

The church is probably unique, and its size and magnificence give some idea of what must have been the importance of the place in the Middle Ages. The town contains numerous interesting buildings; one of which is the old Tolsey House (Plate xcvii). It dates from the fifteenth century, and stands in the centre of the town. It originally stood on stone columns and was open below, but the spaces have been filled in some long time back. The tolls due to the Lord of the Manor, and those incurred by strangers at the fairs, used to be paid in this building, and there still remain in a room upstairs the old chairs, muniment boxes and chest of drawers with the town arms engraved upon them.

The house immediately opposite, of fifteenth century date, is well worth attention, (Plate xcvi), with its three gables, beautiful traceried barge boards, projecting oriel windows, and great pent roof over the shop-fronts below.

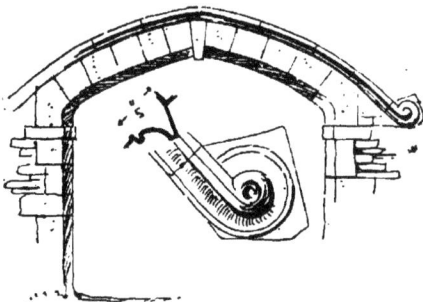

FIG. 82.   ARCHWAY ENTRANCE AT BURFORD.

Inside there is a fine chimney-piece, and, in the courtyard behind, the original wooden windows with arched heads, and a fine timber and plaster front with coved plaster cornice under the eaves.

It was at one time all one house, and the perpendicular windows in the back gable facing the east may have been connected with an oratory chapel on the first floor.

Burford in the time of the Middle Ages must have been full of fascinating buildings, for on all sides are moulded and carved doorways, some of stone and several bearing dates, initials and merchants' marks of the original builders. As a rule the older houses, dating from the time of Henry VIII and Elizabeth, had an arched entrance facing the street, opening into a passage with the rooms leading off it on either side (*see* Fig. 82). This passage further led into a courtyard at the back, and in many of the later buildings the old circular outer staircase, so characteristic of the period, still remains, though generally greatly mutilated.

These courtyards—of which there are many at Campden and Northleach—are delightfully picturesque and are reminiscent of similar instances on the Continent, showing how similar treatments of the same subject produce much the same result in effect, even though executed by different people, hundreds of miles apart. One remarkably fine house, the *Old Bear Inn*, standing in the main street, no doubt owes its name to some connection with the great Earl of Warwick, and there are continuous references to this inn in the Burgesses books from the commencement of the seven-

FIG. 83. ORIEL WINDOW AT BURFORD.

teenth century. It has a beautiful oriel window in the centre of the street front, and though its architectural composition has been much mutilated, enough remains to show what the building was originally like.

Only a short time ago the staircase, enclosed in a circular turret with a high pointed roof, was standing in the large courtyard at the back, but within the last ten years this has unfortunately been pulled down.

All over Burford are typical examples of Cotswold building, and though few are in their original state, even now they are extremely pleasing, and show by what simple and straightforward means such charming effects were gained. To architects the work is especially interesting, for we can see how the different styles and periods overlapped, how traditions lingered, and how loth the builders were to give up accustomed methods. As is the case in all these Cotswold towns and villages, there are many beautiful Renaissance buildings scattered about the streets of Burford, delightful and pleasing touches of a later date, full of charm and simple dignity, and with exquisite detail.

Campden, like Burford, Northleach, and other Cotswold towns, was the abode of rich wool-merchants, who have left behind them lasting traces of their taste, in fine examples of mediaeval art and of their wealth and piety in the fifteenth century church. It is almost unique amongst the many interesting towns, and within its small limits contains some beautiful examples of domestic architecture.

Here we find all styles, from the exquisitely delicate fourteenth century work in the remains of the old town hall, to the stately and scholarly work of Sir Baptist Hicks and the dignified examples of Queen Anne and the early Georges. Small they may be, and perhaps to the passer-by insignificant and hardly noticeable, but all betraying that sense of fitness of purpose and simplicity of expression so characteristic of English architecture at these periods.

We find in Campden the genuine Cotswold commonsense style of building brought almost to perfection, for it lies in the heart of the stone district, and this material is used almost to the exclusion of all others.

Apart from the picturesqueness of its long street, with the somewhat unusual arrangement of groups of isolated buildings, and the strong and sturdy character of its architecture, it is singular in possessing a series of buildings, designed evidently by one hand and erected within a few years of each other.

Though possessing all the charm and variety of the local work, they are stamped with a scholarly feeling and grasp of design and composition that impart an air of distinction apart from the other buildings in the town, and before dealing with them more in detail, a short account of the causes that led to their erection may not be out of place.

As mentioned before, Campden owed its prosperity to its wool trade in the fourteenth and fifteenth centuries, and reached the zenith of its prosperity during the time when England was the great centre and distributor of finished goods all over Europe.

The town has been continuously mentioned by early chroniclers from the seventh century; its historical interest increasing with succeeding years. A search through the Patent Rolls and records reveals many most interesting facts concerning the lives and doings of its inhabitants during the Middle Ages.

In the church there are a series of memorial brasses and tablets to many eminent " woolmen," as they were styled ; amongst others that of William Grevel, citizen of London, " flos mercatorum lanar 'tocuis Anglie," who died in 1401, and his wife Marion in 1386. Part of Grevel's house, built at the close of the fourteenth century, is still standing in the main street, the superb bay window, two storeys in height, so delicately wrought both inside and out, showing the interest and pride that must have been taken in these houses of our forefathers.

After passing through many hands the Manor was bought in 1609 by Sir Baptist Hicks, a wealthy and influential mercer of London, sometime Lord Mayor. He succeeded to his father's business at the sign of the *White Bear* in Cheapside, where he supplied the Court with " silks, satins and rich mercery wares," and in addition made a large fortune through money-lending transactions with the nobility, even extending, so it is said, to the king himself. In 1612 in the height of his prosperity, he bought a large property in Kensington and built himself a town house at Campden Hill, which, after undergoing many vicissitudes, was destroyed by fire in 1862.

In 1613 he commenced to build a large mansion at Campden, on the high ground overlooking the vale to the south of the church, but this also came to the same untimely ending, being unfortunately burnt purposely during the Civil War under the mistaken impression that it would fall into the hands of the Parliamentarians.

Sir Baptist Hicks was raised to the Peerage as Viscount Campden in 1628, and died the following year at another of his London houses in the Old Jewry, and was buried in the South Chapel of Campden Church. He left his two daughters co-heiresses with the enormous fortune (in those days) of £100,000 each. One married Lord Noel, an ancestor of the present Earl Gainsborough, and the other Sir Charles Morison.

When the Civil War broke out the Noels were staunch supporters of the Royalist cause, and Baptist Noel, the third Viscount, raised and kept up at his own expense a regiment of horse and foot soldiers for the service of King Charles I.

F

It would be out of place here to read this page of history and follow his career, intensely interesting as it is, throughout the Civil War, but after being heavily fined and having much property confiscated by the Parliamentarians, he managed to compound for the estate, and eventually died in 1682 and was buried at Exton in Rutlandshire, another of the family seats, where an enormous monument, the work of Nicholas Stone, was erected to his memory in the church.

In the chapel in Campden Church are the several monuments to the Hicks and Noel families, the largest and most striking being that of Sir Baptist Hicks and his wife. It is very elaborate, of black and white marble, finished with pediments and a canopy supported by twelve columns of Egyptian porphyry. Beneath are effigies both lying in their state robes and coronets upon a black marble slab. There is unfortunately no record of either the designer or sculptor of this splendid piece of workmanship.

The chapel also contains many other monuments in the form of effigies and busts, with quaint inscriptions and gorgeously emblazoned coats of arms, all of about the time of Charles I, and apart from their excellent workmanship as examples of the costume of the period, they are well worth noticing.

Sir Baptist Hicks planned his country house on a scale of lavish magnificence even in those opulent days, and with terraces, gardens, fishponds, and extensive outbuildings, it covered a space of over eight acres in extent. Little of the original house remains, excepting the two pavilions at either end of the great terrace, the entrance gateway and the Almonry (Plate xxxii), but these show the fine quality of the work and its peculiar characteristics.

It is to be regretted that the architect of these buildings is unknown, but it is more than probable that Sir Baptist, being one of the wealthiest men of his day, would have employed a man of recognized skill and ability in his profession.

By the same hand are the Almshouses, (Plate x), a simple group of buildings on a raised terrace, overlooking one of the approaches to the great house, and in the main street the beautiful old Market Hall, dated 1627, (Plate xi), still stands as a testimony to the generosity of Sir Baptist and the skill of his architect.

We may in all probability assign to the same man the rebuilding of the church porch, and the conical tops to the staircase turrets leading to the roofs at the N. and S.W. angle of the nave, also the Jacobean pulpit, brass eagle lectern, and many other details in and about the building.

These few buildings are "foreign" in their origin and conception, in the sense that they were not indigenous to the district. They stand apart from the traditional local work and show traces not only of a more trained hand, but also of the Renaissance feeling which was then prevalent in the centres of learning and culture.

Turning to the Market Hall in the main street, we see that it has five arches on either side, with three gables over them, and a wide solid pier beyond, and two arches and gables again at each end of the building, with a series of stone columns inside supporting the roof trusses. There are windows in the gables, originally glazed, but doubtless blocked up in the days of the window-tax. These are too high, and the labels over them too ill-proportioned for the effect to be pleasing.

There is a decided attempt at a classical composition in the arrangement of the arches supporting the architrave, frieze and cornice, which are carried all round the building, with a parapet above, a gutter behind, and lead gargoyles to throw the water into the street below. At one time there was probably a stone balustrade between the arches overlooking the roadway, but a fragment

only now remains.   The mouldings and the stone finials are of a
character quite different to the traditional work of the country,
and a comparison with the building on the other side of the road,
(Plate lxi), almost immediately opposite, will better explain the
difference than any words can do.

The Almshouses, planned in the form of a letter H with an
elongated centre, have precisely
similar details with the unusual
addition of parapets. The delicate
mouldings of the windows, and
labels over, vary from those in the
district, (Figs. 31–33), the centre
mullion of the four-light windows in particular having a circular bead in lieu of the square
fillet.   The panel containing the
coat of arms of the founder both
here, and on the Market Hall is
the same, (Fig. 84), even to the
cutting of the queer little pyramidal ornaments
at either corner.
The carving to
the mantling and
crest is done with
a vigour and feel-
ing quite beyond that seen in purely local work.

FIG. 84. COAT OF ARMS ON THE
MARKET HALL, CHIPPING CAMPDEN.

FIG. 85. STRINGS
AT THE
"KITE'S NEST,"
CAMPDEN.

The small building, (Pl. xxxii), one of many of those in connection with the great house, shows in its mouldings and general
character a close relationship with the other buildings, the string
courses being identical and the arrangement of the chimneys with the

gable between them, the moulded caps and shafts being the same as those to the almshouses.

Some few miles distant there is a house called the Kite's Nest, which again contains all the peculiarities of detail just referred to, (*see* Fig. 85), and as these are quite unusual in this district, it is perhaps not too hasty a conclusion to draw, that they were all done within a few years of each other and by the same hand.

There are numerous other buildings in Campden which merit more than a passing glance, many of these much later in date, but all containing some detail or characteristic rather out of the common. Look for instance at the house in the main street dated 1705 (Plate ix). This was the period when the fine panelled white rooms of Queen Anne's reign had usurped the place of the low beamed ceilings of the preceding century. We see in the main features of the outward shell the local traditions sti l adhered to, but the mullioned windows have now a transome and upper lights, though still moulded exactly the same as before. The four-centred doorway is the old form, but instead of the hollow label, we have a delicately moulded cornice and broken pediment showing at a glance the influence, even in these remote parts, of Wren and his school. There is a moulded cornice over the windows and under the eaves of the roof a stone cove. With the exception of these later innovations all else is in the local style, and this house, which is a type of many others scattered about these Cotswold towns, is to architects particularly interesting as showing how the new ideas were grafted on to the older forms.

In the street view, (Plate xcviii), the house in the foreground, which has been much altered in the course of its existence, has a fine gable of somewhat unusual width, not particularly noticeable in itself, except for the arrangement on either side. At the springing of the gable there are two moulded and carved square pedestals, supporting smaller circular vases (*see* Fig. 86). These are in stone, but planted in each is a tulip flower, with leaves and stalks, daintily wrought in iron, a quaint and pleasing conceit which is quite unique in this part of England.

FIG. 86.   GABLE AT CAMPDEN.

It is impossible to do more than touch upon the most salient features of these Cotswold houses, but an endeavour has been made to show that in these quiet villages and hamlets work still exists as good and truthful as that which we all so admire in other and more populous parts of the country. We are apt to forget that it is in these villages the history of our country life is written, and that the sturdy yeomen who built these houses and quarried the stone and cut the timber with their own hands, formed a distinct style of architecture.

To-day such buildings are out of the question, for the conditions of life and of labour throughout the whole country are changed, and though this may be a matter for regret, yet it is impossible to revert to the old ways.

But we can gain many valuable lessons from a study of these old buildings, and one is that the necessity of using only the materials to hand contributed greatly to the restfulness of the old work.

There are very few country districts in England that do not possess much beautiful local material, be it stone, or brick, flint or chalk, that is far more suited to its surroundings than strange importations out of harmony with the locality. Modern building suffers because architects do not sufficiently rely upon the use of the materials of the districts they are building in.

Years ago, and to a certain extent even to-day, one could tell by glancing at a building, not only the character of the local materials, but almost the particular district of England in which it was built; each neighbourhood was stamped with its special features, not of style or date, but of material, which in its own particular vernacular, spoke eloquently a language not to be mistaken or confused with that of any other part of the country.

To-day all this delightful tradition seems to be abandoned, and we use all sorts of materials, regardless of their appropriateness, in every part of the country—green Westmorland slates in Kent, red tile hanging in the heart of stone districts, and stone houses in the places where stone is not.

Consequently there is a feeling of unrestfulness pervading

much of the country building of to-day, and it does not seem to fit either its occupants or its surroundings.

In face of the fact that such beautiful work has been done in the past, there is no sound reason for the introduction of " foreign " materials, and to break entirely with the traditional use of local ones, which is now so often done, seems quite unnecessary. Of course it will be urged that expense is the chief obstacle; but the fact that in many parts of England their use has been neglected for so many years, not only adds to the cost, but renders their employment to-day a matter of great difficulty.

Those who build should try to foster and encourage all local crafts and industries, as they are rapidly dying out for want of employment, and it will soon be too late to bring them into use again.

New buildings should be designed in as modern a spirit as we wish, but using the materials at hand. The very fact that in so doing we shall be more or less governed by the same conditions and limitations as these old builders, will give our work to-day a continuity in design and feeling, in harmony with the old, and will help to carry on in a certain sense the spirit and tradition of bygone days, which surely in these times of change and hurry, will appeal to many.

Butler & Tanner, The Selwood Printing Works, Frome, and London.

Plate I.

A FARMHOUSE AT STANTON, GLOS.

Plate II.

A FARMHOUSE AT WILLERSEY, GLOS.

Plate III.

COTTAGE WITH PORCH, LITTLE RISSINGTON, GLOS.

COTTAGES AT STANTON, GLOS.

Plate V.

A FARMHOUSE AT WILLERSEY, GLOS.

COTTAGES AT COLN ST. ALDWYN, GLOS.

A HOUSE AT WESTON SUBEDGE, GLOS.

Plate VIII.

AT CHALFORD HILL, NEAR STROUD, GLOS.

Plate IX.

HOUSE IN THE HIGH STREET, CAMPDEN, GLOS.

THE ALMSHOUSES, CAMPDEN, GLOS.

Plate XI.

THE MARKET HALL, CAMPDEN, GLOS.

THE SWAN INN, HARRINGWORTH, NORTHANTS.

Plate XIII.

STREET FRONT OF A FARMHOUSE, LITTLE RISSINGTON, GLOS.

Plate XIV

BACK OF A FARMHOUSE, LITTLE RISSINGTON, GLOS.

Plate XV.

A FARMHOUSE AT GRETTON, NORTHANTS.

Plate XVI.

COTTAGES AT CHEDWORTH, GLOS.

Plate XVII.

COTTAGES AT FINSTOCK, OXON.

Plate XVIII.

A COTTAGE AT FINSTOCK, OXON.

Plate XIX.

THE POST OFFICE, DUCKLINGTON, OXON.

Plate XX.

COTTAGES AT GRETTON, NORTHANTS.

Plate XXI.

THE MANOR HOUSE, GRETTON, NORTHANTS.

Plate XXII.

A COTTAGE AT BLISWORTH, NORTHANTS.

Plate XXIII.

COTTAGES AT AWKWARD HILL, ARLINGTON, GLOS.

Plate XXIV.

A COTTAGE AT BIBURY, GLOS.

.

Plate XXV.

TUDOR HOUSE, MICKLETON, GLOS.

Plate XXVI.

A HOUSE AT SNOWSHILL, GLOS.

VIEW IN THE VILLAGE STREET, BROADWAY, WORC.

THE VILLAGE CROSS AND A COTTAGE, STANTON, GLOS.

Plate XXIX.

THE GROCER'S SHOP, COLLEY WESTON, NORTHANTS.

Plate XXX.

TOP FARM, BROADWAY, WORC.

TOP FARM, BROADWAY, WORC.

Plate XXXII.

THE "ALMONRY," CAMPDEN, GLOS.

Plate XXXIII.

A COTTAGE AT STANWAY, GLOS.

Plate XXXIV.

A FARMHOUSE AT LAVERTON, NEAR BROADWAY, GLOS.

Plate XXXV.

BACK OF A FARMHOUSE, LAVERTON, NEAR BROADWAY, GLOS.

Plate XXXVI.

A FARMHOUSE AT SAINTBURY, GLOS.

Plate XXXVII.

A STREET VIEW, PAINSWICK, GLOS.

Plate XXXVIII.

HOUSES AT WESTON SU'BEDGE, GLOS.

Plate XXXIX.

WARREN HOUSE, STANTON, GLOS.

Plate XL.

DOORWAY AT WARREN HOUSE, STANTON, GLOS.

Plate XLI.

A COTTAGE AT CHALFORD HILL, NEAR STROU'D, GLOS.

Plate XLII.

A COTTAGE AT LILFIELD, NEAR STROUD, GLOS.

DOORWAY AT BOWMEADOW FARM, LAVERTON, NEAR BROADWAY, GLOS.

HOUSE IN ST. PAUL'S STREET, STAMFORD, NORTHANTS.

IN CHURCH STREET, STROUD, GLOS.

A STREET VIEW AT CIRENCESTER, GLOS.

Plate XLVII.

A SMALL HOUSE AT WITHINGTON, GLOS.

Plate XLVIII.

THE MANOR FARM, RAMSDEN, OXON.

Plate XLIX.

COTTAGES AT WESTON SUBEDGE, GLOS.

Plate I.

THE VILLAGE SCHOOL, ASTON SUBEDGE, GLOS.

Plate LI.

THE VILLAGE SCHOOL, ASTON SUBEDGE, GLOS.

THE COURT FARM, BROADWAY, WORC.

Plate LIII

ST. EDWARD'S GRAMMAR SCHOOL, STOW-ON-THE-WOLD, GLOS.

THE SOUTH FRONT, MANOR FARM, TEMPLE GUITING, GLOS.

Plate LV.

END OF SOUTH FRONT, MANOR FARM, TEMPLE GUITING, GLOS.

THE SCHOOL HOUSE, BAMPTON, OXON.

COTTAGES AT YARWELL, NORTHANTS.

.

Plate LVIII.

A COTTAGE AT DUDDINGTON, NORTHANTS.

Plate LIX.

COTTAGES AT CHIPPING CAMPDEN, GLOS.

Plate LX.

THE SWAN INN, LECHLADE, GLOS.

Plate LXI.

A STREET HOUSE IN CAMPDEN, GLOS.

Plate LXII.

THE PLOUGH INN, CALLOWELL, NEAR STROUD, GLOS.

Plate LXIII.

A FARMHOUSE AT NASSINGTON, NORTHANTS.

Plate LXIV.

A FARMHOUSE AT BARFORD, OXON.

.

Plate LXV.

A GABLE FROM LYDDINGTON, RUTLAND.

Plate LXVI.

A HOUSE AT BOURTON-ON-THE-WATER, GLOS.

Plate LXVII.

A COTTAGE AT NASSINGTON, NORTHANTS.

Plate LXVIII.

COTTAGES AT WESTON SUBEDGE, GLOS.

Plate LXIX.

A COTTAGE WITH DORMER AT STANTON, GLOS.

A GROUP OF COTTAGES, BIBURY, GLOS.

Plate LXXII.

THE MANOR HOUSE, WITHINGTON, GLOS.

Plate LXXIII.

A COTTAGE AT CHURCH ICCOMB, GLOS.

BACK OF AN INN, NEAR STROUD, GLOS.

Plate LXXV.

DEAN ROW, COLN ST. ALDWYN, GLOS.

Plate LXXVI.

A COTTAGE WINDOW, BROADWAY, WORC.

Plate LXXVII.

THE BAKER'S HOUSE, BOURTON-ON-THE-HILL, GLOS.

Plate LXXVIII.

THE CARPENTER'S SHOP, BOURTON-ON-THE-HILL, GLOS.

Plate LXXIX.

A FARMHOUSE AT PAXFORD, GLOS.

FRONT VIEW OF MEDFORD HOUSE, MICKLETON, GLOS.

Plate LXXXI.

THE ENTRANCE, MEDFORD HOUSE, MICKLETON, GLOS.

Plate LXXXII.

EAST END OF MEDFORD HOUSE, MICKLETON, GLOS.

Plate LXXXIII.

THE KITCHEN CHIMNEY, MEDFORD HOUSE, MICKLETON, GLOS.

Plate LXXXIV.

THE VILLAGE INN, WILLERSEY, GLOS.

Plate LXXXV.

COTTAGES AT EBRINGTON, GLOS.

HUMPHRIES END FARM, NEAR STROUD, GLOS.

Plate LXXXVII.

A COTTAGE AT WOODCHESTER, NEAR STROUD, GLOS.

COTTAGES AT LAVERTON, NEAR BROADWAY, GLOS.

Plate LXXXIX.

COTTAGES AT PAINSWICK, GLOS.

Plate XC.

THE RECTORY, COLN ROGER, GLOS.

Plate XCI.

A HOUSE AT CHEDWORTH, GLOS.

.

Plate XCII.

THE BULL AND SWAN INN, STAMFORD, NORTHANTS.

Plate XCIII.

THE WHITE LION INN, OUNDLE, NORTHANTS.

CALLOWELL FARM, NEAR STROUD, GLOS.

Plate XCV

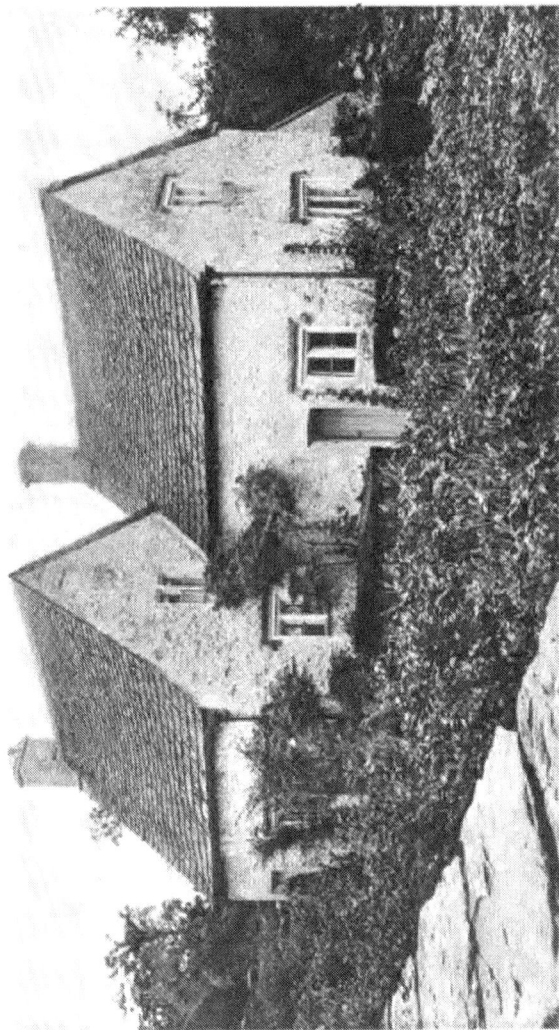

COTTAGES AT CHEDWORTH, GLOS.

A HOUSE IN THE HIGH STREET, BURFORD, OXON.

.

Plate XCVII.

THE TOLSEY, HIGH STREET, BURFORD, OXON.

Plate XCVIII.

THE MAIN STREET, CAMPDEN, GLOS.

Plate XCIX.

AT WESTINGTON, NEAR CAMPDEN, GLOS.

Plate C.

A FARMHOUSE AT LEONARD STANLEY, NEAR STROUD, GLOS.

A List of Standard Books on

ARCHITECTURE & ART, BUILDING, ETC.

Published & sold by B. T. BATSFORD
94, HIGH HOLBORN, LONDON.

Large crown 8vo, cloth, gilt. 5s. *net.*

ESSENTIALS IN ARCHITECTURE. An Analysis of the Principles and Qualities to be looked for in Buildings. By JOHN BELCHER, A.R.A., Fellow and Past President of the Royal Institute of British Architects. With about 80 illustrations (mostly full-page) of Old and Modern Buildings.

Mr. R. NORMAN SHAW, R.A., writes:—"I have read the proofs of this work with the greatest interest. I am quite sure it will arouse enthusiasm in hundreds of readers, but if it attracted only a dozen, it would not have been written in vain. Mr. Belcher wishes his readers to think of Architecture—architecturally ; tells them how to do so, and no one is more competent to teach them."

Imperial 8vo, cloth, gilt. 31s. 6d: *net.*

GOTHIC ARCHITECTURE IN ENGLAND. An Analysis of the Origin and Development of English Church Architecture, from the Norman Conquest to the Dissolution of the Monasteries. By FRANCIS BOND, M.A., Hon.A.R.I.B.A. Containing 750 pages, with 1,254 Illustrations from photographs, measured drawings, and sketches, including 20 full-page Collotypes and 469 of plans, sections, diagrams, and moldings.

" The fullest and most complete illustrated treatise on the subject which has yet appeared. . . . . It is a book which every student of architecture, professional or amateur, ought to have."—*The Builder.*
" A truly monumental work . . . . profusely illustrated. . . . . As a mine of erudition, of detailed analysis and information, and of criticism, the book is worthy of all praise."—*The Times.*
" Perfectly orderly, and most complete and thorough, this great book leaves nothing to be desired."—*The Building News.*
"This is, in every sense of the word, a great book. . . . . It is a book that at once steps to the front as authoritative, and it will be long before it is superseded."—*The Athenæum.*

Large 8vo, cloth, gilt. 18s. *net.*

THE ARCHITECTURE OF GREECE AND ROME. A SKETCH OF ITS HISTORIC DEVELOPMENT. By WILLIAM J. ANDERSON, Author of "The Architecture of the Renaissance in Italy," and R. PHENÉ SPIERS, F.S.A. Second Edition, revised and much enlarged. With 250 Illustrations from photographs and drawings, including many full-page Plates, of which 24 are finely printed in Collotype.

" As a comprehensive *résumé* of the history and characteristics of Greek and Roman architecture this must certainly be considered to be the best one-volume work of its kind that has yet appeared in our language."—*The Builder.*
" A vivid and scholarly picture of Classic Art."—*The British Architect.*
" It is such a work as many students of Architecture and the Classics have vainly yearned or, and lost precious years in supplying its place."—*The Architect.*

D. 9. 07.

2 vols., large folio, half morocco, gilt. £8 8s. net.

LATER RENAISSANCE ARCHITECTURE IN ENGLAND.
A Series of Examples of the Domestic Buildings erected sub-
sequent to the Elizabethan Period. Edited, with Introductory
and Descriptive Text, by JOHN BELCHER, A.R.A., and
MERVYN E. MACARTNEY, F.R.I.B.A. Containing 170 magnifi-
cent Plates (19 ins. × 14 ins.), 130 of which are reproduced in
Collotype from photographs specially taken, and 40 from
measured drawings by various accomplished draughtsmen. With
153 further Illustrations of plans, details, &c., in the letterpress.

"One of the most remarkable and fascinating works in architectural illustration which has
appeared in our time."—*The Builder.*
"A very sumptuous and beautiful publication."—*The Architectural Review.*
"Every admirer of the Renaissance in this country should possess a copy of this work."—*The
Building News.*

2 vols., large folio, half morocco, gilt. £8 8s. net.

ARCHITECTURE OF THE RENAISSANCE IN ENGLAND.
Illustrated by a Series of Views and Details from Buildings
erected between the years 1560 and 1635, with Historical and
Critical Text. By J. ALFRED GOTCH, F.S.A., F.R.I.B.A.
Containing 145 folio Plates (size 19 ins. × 14 ins.), 118 being
reproduced from Photographs taken expressly for the work and
27 from measured drawings, with 180 further Illustrations of
plans, details, &c., in the Text.

"The volumes are very beautiful in themselves, and a striking proof of the almost unknown
wealth of domestic architecture of ancient date in which England stands alone."—*The Times.*

Large 8vo, cloth, gilt. £1 1s. net.

EARLY RENAISSANCE ARCHITECTURE IN ENGLAND.
An Historical and Descriptive Account of the Tudor, Eliza-
bethan and Jacobean Periods, 1500—1625. By J. ALFRED
GOTCH, F.S.A. With 87 Collotype and other Plates and 230
Illustrations in the Text, from Drawings by various accom-
plished Draughtsmen, and from photographs specially taken.

"A more delightful book for the architect it would be hard to find. It is quite a storehouse
of references and illustrations, and should be quite indispensable to the architect's library."—
The British Architect.

Large folio, cloth, gilt. £1 10s. net.

SOME ARCHITECTURAL WORKS OF INIGO JONES.
Illustrated by a Series of Measured Drawings of the Chief
Buildings designed by him, together with Descriptive and Bio-
graphical Notes, and a complete List of his Authentic Works.
By H. INIGO TRIGGS and HENRY TANNER, AA.R.I.B.A.
Containing 40 Plates and numerous Illustrations in the Text.

"The plates are quite perfect as specimens of draughtsmanship, and possess a crispness and
freedom of handling which differentiate them from ordinary measured drawings."—*A. A. Notes.*
"The authors have illustrated all that they have found good reason to regard as Jones's work,
and their capitally produced volume forms a worthy addition to the history of the Later
Renaissance in England."—*The Building News.*

Thick demy 8vo, cloth, gilt. £1 1s. net.

A HISTORY OF ARCHITECTURE on the Comparative Method for the Student, Craftsman, and Amateur. By Professor BANISTER FLETCHER, F.R.I.B.A., and BANISTER F. FLETCHER, F.R.I.B.A. Fifth Edition, revised and greatly enlarged by BANISTER F. FLETCHER. With about 2,000 Illustrations, reproduced from Photographs of Buildings of all Ages, and from specially prepared Drawings of Constructive and Ornamental Detail.

"*Par excellence* the student's manual of the history of architecture."—*The Architect.*
"A complete, trustworthy, and extremely attractive manual."—*The Builder.*
"Immeasurably superior to the original edition. . . ."—*The Architectural Review.*

3 vols., large 8vo, cloth, gilt. £3 15s. net.

A HISTORY OF ARCHITECTURE, having special regard to the natural artistic results of Construction and those Methods of Design which are the result of abstract thinking and of the pure sense of form. By RUSSELL STURGIS, M.A., Ph.D., Editor of "A Dictionary of Architecture and Building," Author of "European Architecture," "How to Judge Architecture," etc.

This important work will be completed in three volumes, the first of which is now published. Each volume will contain about 500 pages, with some 350 full-page and smaller illustrations, reproduced in collotype, half-tone, and line, from special photographs and drawings; the whole produced in the best possible manner. Volumes 2 and 3 will appear during 1908.

Large 8vo, cloth, gilt. 12s. 6d. net.

THE ARCHITECTURE OF THE RENAISSANCE IN ITALY. A General View for the use of Students and Others. By WILLIAM J. ANDERSON, A.R.I.B.A. Third Edition, with 64 full-page Collotype and other Plates, and nearly 100 smaller Illustrations in the text, from photographs and drawings.

"Mr. Anderson's book is of the greatest value, and enables the student, for the first time, to grasp the true significance of the movement."—*The Builder's Journal.*
"The book is evidence of earnest study."—*The Architect.*
"Should rank amongst the best architectural writings of the day."—*The Edinburgh Review.*

Large 8vo, cloth. 7s. 6d. net.

HOW TO JUDGE ARCHITECTURE. A Popular Guide to the Appreciation of Buildings. By RUSSELL STURGIS, M.A. With 84 full-page Illustrations, reproduced in half-tone, from photographs of some of the chief buildings of the world.

"It contains for the layman an education in architecture."—*The Lamp, New York.*

Large 8vo, cloth. 7s. 6d. net.

THE APPRECIATION OF SCULPTURE. A Popular Handbook for Students and Amateurs. By RUSSELL STURGIS, M.A. With 64 full-page Illustrations, reproduced in half-tone, from photographs of some of the most notable examples of the art.

"This interesting volume, with its admirably chosen illustrations, its skilful criticisms, and its cultured survey of the history of the art, cannot but prove helpful to any reader who wishes to form well-reasoned opinions on its subject."—*The Scotsman.*

B. T. BATSFORD,
PUBLISHER,
94, High Holborn, London.

2 vols., royal 4to, half bound. £2 2s. net. (Published at £5 5s.)
ANCIENT DOMESTIC ARCHITECTURE IN GREAT
BRITAIN. By F. T. DOLLMAN, Architect. Containing 161
beautiful Lithographic Plates, illustrating by means of careful
measured drawings and sketches the principal examples of
Mediæval Domestic Architecture in England, with Analytical
and Descriptive Text.

"Mr. Dollman's is the best illustrated and most generally useful book on the *civil* architecture of the Middle Ages. The buildings here drawn and described comprise not only dwelling-houses of varying degrees of importance—from the mansion of a lord-of-the-manor or merchant-prince to the cottage of a small tradesman in a country town—but also palaces, colleges, halls, schools, hospitals, and almshouses."—*Arthur S. Flower, M.A., F.S.A., A.R.I.B.A.*

2 vols., royal 4to, cloth, gilt. £2 2s. net. (Published at £5 5s.)
DETAILS OF GOTHIC ARCHITECTURE, measured and
drawn from Existing Examples of the XIIth, XIIIth, XIVth,
and XVth Centuries, by J. K. COLLING, Architect. Containing
190 Lithographed Plates, chiefly of measured drawings.

"Mr. Colling's beautiful and accurate records of a great architectural epoch and of the indigenous art of this country have an inherent value and interest which can never entirely disappear. The illustrations offer invaluable assistance towards understanding and comparing the various phases of Gothic design, from the general lines of composition down to the most minute details of construction and of ornamentation."—*Arthur S. Flower, Esq., M.A., F.S.A.*

Royal 4to, cloth, gilt. 15s. net. (Published at £2 2s.)
MEDIÆVAL FOLIAGE AND COLOURED DECORATION
IN ENGLAND. By JAS. K. COLLING. A series of Examples
taken from Buildings of the Twelfth to the Fifteenth Century.
Containing 76 Lithographic Plates, representing 600 examples.

A book of exceptional and very nearly unique interest. Apart from
Pugin's "Gothic Ornaments," it is the only collection that exists of well-
drawn specimens of old English carved work, both in *stone and wood, and
ranging over the whole of the Middle Ages.*

Large 4to, art canvas, gilt. £1 15s. net.
THE ART AND CRAFT OF GARDEN MAKING. By
THOMAS H. MAWSON, Garden Architect. Third Edition,
revised and much enlarged. Containing upwards of 300
Illustrations (many being full-page) of perspective views,
plans, and details of gardens, ranging in size from a tiny
cottage garden to gardens of twelve acres in extent.

Folio, half morocco, gilt. £4 4s. net.
FORMAL GARDENS IN ENGLAND AND SCOTLAND.
A Series of Views, Plans and Details of the finest Old Gardens
still existing. With an Introduction and Descriptive Accounts.
By H. INIGO TRIGGS, A.R.I.B.A. Containing 125 fine Plates,
72 from the Author's Drawings, and 53 from Photographs
specially taken.

"That the book will make a charming addition to the libraries of artistic-minded people
there can be no doubt whatever, and to the lover of gardens, from an architect's point of view
particularly, we can hardly imagine a more welcome or elegant publication."—*The Building News.*

Crown 4to, handsomely bound in art canvas, gilt. Price 21s. each, net.

OLD ENGLISH COTTAGES AND FARM-HOUSES.

A Series of Volumes designed to illustrate the most typical and beautiful remains of minor Domestic Architecture in England. Each volume contains 100 Photographic Plates, artistically printed in Collotype, accompanied by Descriptive Notes and Sketches.

(1) KENT AND SUSSEX. Photographed by W. GALSWORTHY DAVIE and described by E. GUY DAWBER. The rural buildings of Kent and Sussex are typical of native homely English work, and amongst them may be found nearly every style of architecture.

" Every cottage illustrated has interest through its picturesqueness, and the variety of them is remarkable."—*The Architect.*
" All lovers of our domestic architecture should buy this book."—*The Antiquary.*

(2) SHROPSHIRE, HEREFORDSHIRE, AND CHESHIRE. Photographed by JAMES PARKINSON and described by E. A. OULD. This volume illustrates the half-timber buildings characteristic of these counties.

"No districts in Great Britain are more richly endowed with specimens of genuine half-timber work than these three beautifully wooded counties, so that Mr. Parkinson has had little difficulty in providing an attractive series of photographs in his well-produced and useful volume."—*The Building News.*

(3) THE COTSWOLD DISTRICT, comprising parts of Gloucestershire, Oxfordshire, Northants, and Worcestershire. Photographed by W. GALSWORTHY DAVIE and described by E. GUY DAWBER. The buildings illustrated in this volume are essentially of a stone type, and present a special variety of architecture, very dissimilar to those illustrated in the two previous volumes.

"This charming volume contains one hundred photographs of the most beautiful domestic buildings in the country . . . ."—*The Daily News.*

Large 8vo, art canvas, gilt. 15s. net.

OLD ENGLISH DOORWAYS. A Series of Historical Examples from Tudor Times to the end of the XVIIIth Century. Illustrated on 70 Plates, reproduced in Collotype from Photographs specially taken by W. GALSWORTHY DAVIE. With Historical and Descriptive Notes on the subjects, including 34 Drawings and Sketches by HENRY TANNER, A.R.I.B.A., Author of " English Interior Woodwork."

" A most admirable addition to any library of architectural and artistic books. The subjects brought together in this volume comprise many of the best types of doorways to be seen in England."—*The Building News.*

B. T. BATSFORD,
PUBLISHER,
94, High Holborn, London.

Imperial 4to, cloth. 10s. 6d.

ORDERS OF ARCHITECTURE — Greek, Roman, and
Italian. A Collection of Typical Examples from Normand's
"Parallels" and other Authorities, with Notes on the Origin
and Development of the Classic Orders, and descriptions of
the plates, by R. Phené Spiers, F.S.A., Master of the
Architectural School of the Royal Academy. Fourth Edition,
revised and enlarged, containing 27 full-page Plates, seven of
which have been specially prepared for the work.

"A most useful work for architectural students, clearly setting forth in comparative form the
various orders. Mr. Spiers gives recognised examples of the principal forms of capital and base,
and of the finer and bolder profiles of entablatures, with their decorative complements. A good
feature of the plates is the scale below each in English feet. Mr. Spiers's notes are also very
appropriate and useful."—*The British Architect.*
"An indispensable possession to all students of architecture."—*The Architect.*

Folio, in strong portfolio. 12s. 6d. net.

EXAMPLES OF CLASSIC ORNAMENT FROM GREECE
AND ROME. Drawn from the originals by Lewis Vulliamy.
A Re-issue, containing 20 selected plates (size 19½ ins. ×
13½ ins.), illustrating a choice collection of examples, with
Descriptive Notes, by R. Phené Spiers, F.S.A., F.R.I.B.A.

This volume contains a selection of the most characteristic and useful
plates from the rare folio work of Vulliamy, first published in 1825, and
long since out of print and practically unobtainable. The plates display in
their spirited execution an intimate appreciation of the refinement and
vigour which characterises the best work in Athens and Rome, and to
architectural students requiring authoritative and well-drawn illustrations
they will be invaluable.

Small folio, cloth, gilt. £1 5s. net.

THE HISTORIC STYLES OF ORNAMENT. Containing
1,500 Examples of the Ornament of all Countries and Periods,
exhibited in 100 Plates, mostly printed in Gold and Colours.
With Historical and Descriptive Text (containing 136 Illustrations), translated from the German of H. Dolmetsch.

A well-selected "Grammar of Ornament," which gives particular
attention to the Art of the Renaissance.

Royal 8vo, cloth, gilt. 6s. net.

A MANUAL OF HISTORIC ORNAMENT. Treating upon the
Evolution, Tradition, and Development of Architecture and
other Applied Arts. Prepared for the use of Students and
Craftsmen. By Richard Glazier, A.R.I.B.A., Headmaster
of the Manchester School of Art. Second edition, revised and
enlarged, containing 600 Illustrations drawn by the author.

"Not since the publication of Owen Jones' celebrated 'Grammar of Ornament' have we
seen any book, brought out on popular lines, that could compare with Mr. Glazier's 'Manual.
In many ways it is the better book of the two. . . . It simply abounds with beautiful,
delicately-drawn illustrations, and forms a perfect treasury of designs."—*The Bookseller.*
"It would be difficult, if not wellnigh impossible, to find a more useful and comprehensive
book than this, which contains examples of all the leading groups of ornamental design, and many
more minor ones, but invariably interesting and valuable."—*The Athenæum.*

Thick demy 8vo, cloth, gilt.   12s. 6d.

A HANDBOOK OF ORNAMENT. With 3,000 Illustrations of the Elements and the Application of Decoration to Objects. By F. S. MEYER, Professor at the School of Applied Art, Karlsruhe. 3rd English Edition, revised by HUGH STANNUS, F.R.I.B.A., Hon. A.R.C.A.

"A LIBRARY, A MUSEUM, AN ENCYCLOPÆDIA, AND AN ART SCHOOL IN ONE. TO RIVAL IT AS A BOOK OF REFERENCE ONE MUST FILL A BOOKCASE."—*The Studio.*

Demy 8vo, art linen, gilt.   6s. net.

THE PRINCIPLES OF DESIGN. · A Textbook especially designed to meet the requirements of the Board of Education Examination Syllabus on " Principles of Ornament." By G. WOOLLISCROFT RHEAD, Hon. A.R.C.A. With 16 photographic plates and over 400 other Illustrations, chiefly from line drawings.

Crown 8vo, cloth.   3s. 6d. net.

ALPHABETS, OLD AND NEW. Containing 200 complete Alphabets, 30 Series of Numerals, Numerous Facsimiles of Ancient Dates, &c. Selected and arranged by LEWIS F. DAY. Preceded by a short account of the Development of the Alphabet. Second Edition, revised and Enlarged, with many further Examples. The most handy, useful, and comprehensive work on the subject.

"Everyone who employs practical lettering will be grateful for ' Alphabets, Old and New.' Mr. Day has written a scholarly and pithy introduction, and contributes some beautiful alphabets of his own design."—*The Art Journal.*

Crown 8vo, cloth.   5s. net.

LETTERING IN ORNAMENT. An Enquiry into the Decorative Use of Lettering, Past, Present, and Possible. By LEWIS F. DAY. With 200 Illustrations from Photographs and Drawings.

"The book itself is an admirable one, and the author's clearness of thought and expression makes it most readable and instructive. . . . The illustrations range over a wide field and are invaluable, as they show at once what has been done by the artists of many nations."—*The Builder's Journal.*

Crown 8vo, cloth.   5s. net.

ART IN NEEDLEWORK : A BOOK ABOUT EMBROIDERY. By LEWIS F. DAY and MARY BUCKLE. Second Edition, revised, containing 80 full-page Plates, reproduced from photographs, and 45 Illustrations in the text.

An invaluable Review of the Art and Practice of Embroidery.

Demy 8vo, cloth, gilt, price (about) 6s. 6d. net.

ENAMELLING. A Comparative Account of the Development and Practice of the Art. For the Use of Artists, Craftsmen, Students, &c. By LEWIS F. DAY. With 115 Illustrations, reproduced from special drawings and photographs.

[Ready in November, 1907.

This volume will form a very comprehensive survey of the course of enamelling, both as an art in itself and as a branch of the jeweller's craft. The book should appeal to all who practise enamelling, and to those who only take an interest in it.

B. T. BATSFORD,
PUBLISHER,
94. High Holborn, London.

MR. LEWIS F. DAY'S HANDBOOKS of ORNAMENTAL DESIGN.

Demy 8vo, cloth, gilt.   7s. 6d. net.

PATTERN DESIGN. A Book for Students, treating in a prac-
tical way of the Anatomy, Planning, and Evolution of Repeated
Ornament. Containing 300 pages of text, with upwards of 300
Illustrations, reproduced from drawings and from photographs.

"Every line and every illustration in this book should be studied carefully and continually
by everyone having any aspiration toward designing."—*The Decorator.*

Demy 8vo, cloth, gilt.   8s. 6d. net.

ORNAMENT AND ITS APPLICATION. A sequel to "Pattern
Design," and an Introduction to the Study of Design in relation
to Material, Tools, and ways of Workmanship. Containing 320
pages, with 300 Illustrations of Decorative Objects and Ornament, reproduced from Photographs and Drawings.

Mr. Walter Crane, writing in the "Manchester Guardian," says : " . . . The
work can be confidently commended as a most workmanlike and accomplished treatise not
only to all students of design, but to artists and craftsmen generally. The illustrations are
extremely rich and varied."

"It bears the unmistakable impress of originality and practical ability. . . . . It deals
with its subject far more fully than any previous publication, whilst the numerous excellent
illustrations will be an invaluable aid to teacher and student."—*The Studio.*

Thick crown 8vo, cloth, gilt.   12s. 6d.

NATURE IN ORNAMENT. An Enquiry into the Natural
Element in Ornamental Design, and a Survey of the Ornamental Treatment of Natural Forms. With 450 Illustrations.
3rd Edition, revised and enlarged.

"A book more beautiful for its illustrations or one more useful to students of art can hardly
be imagined."—*The Queen.*

Medium 8vo, cloth, gilt.   £1 1s. net.

WINDOWS: A BOOK ABOUT STAINED AND PAINTED
GLASS. By LEWIS F. DAY. Second Edition, revised, containing 50 full-page Plates, and upwards of 200 other Illustrations.

"Contains a more complete account—technical and historical—of stained and painted glass
than has previously appeared in this country."—*The Times.*

" Mr. Day has done a worthy piece of work in more than his usual admirable manner. . . .
The illustrations are all good, and some the best black-and-white drawings of stained glass yet
produced."—*The Studio.*

Demy 8vo, cloth, gilt, price (about) 12s. 6d. net.

HERALDRY AS ART. An Account of its Development and
Practice, chiefly in England. By GEORGE W. EVE, R.E.
With 300 Illustrations of typical heraldic design, old and new.

[Ready in No. ber, 1907.

SUMMARY OF CONTENTS.—The Origin, Uses, and Aims of Heraldry—
The Evolution of Shield Forms—Heraldic Rules—Animals and Monsters
—Heraldic Birds and other Figures — Helm, Crest, and Mantling—
Armorial Accessories—Methods and Materials—Architectural Decoration—
Embroidered Heraldry—Some Miscellaneous Charges—Marks of Cadency.

Large 8vo, cloth. 5s. net.

A HANDBOOK OF PLANT FORM FOR STUDENTS OF
DESIGN. By ERNEST E. CLARK, Art Master, Derby Tech-
nical College. Containing 100 Plates (size 10½ ins. by 7½ ins.),
illustrating 61 varieties of Plants, comprising 800 Illustrations.
With an Introductory Chapter on the Elementary Principles of
Design, Notes on the Plants, and a Glossary of Botanical Terms.

"Such a book has long been needed, and the appearance of this handsome volume at such a
moderate price will be hailed with satisfaction by students of design everywhere."—*Arts and
Crafts.*

Imperial 4to, handsomely bound in cloth gilt. £1 5s. net.

DECORATIVE FLOWER STUDIES for the use of Artists,
Designers, Students and others. By J. FOORD. A series of
40 full-page Plates, coloured in facsimile of the Author's
original water-colour drawings, accompanied by 350 Studies
of Detail showing the Development of the Plant in successive
stages. With Descriptive Notes.

"A truly valuable and beautiful book. . . . . The coloured plates are nearly all good :
they have a certain spaciousness of treatment that is full of delicacy and freedom ; and we have
no doubt at all that the book, considered as a whole, is a real gain to all who take delight in the
decorative representation of flowers."—*The Studio.*

Imperial 4to, handsomely bound in cloth, gilt. £1 10s. net.

DECORATIVE PLANT AND FLOWER STUDIES. For the
Use of Artists, Designers, Students, and others. By J. FOORD.
Containing 40 full-page Plates, coloured in facsimile, of the
Author's original Water-Colour Drawings, with a Description
and Sketch of each plant, and 450 Studies of growth and detail.

"Never before has the essential character of different plants received from the point of view of
their adaptability for decorative purposes the careful study and brilliant representation which they
receive at Miss Foord's hands in this exquisitely printed and coloured book."—*Daily Telegraph.*
"Alike to the lover of nature and the student of design, this volume will prove a rich fund of
delight and instruction."—*The Queen.*

Crown 8vo, cloth. 3s. 6d. net.

DECORATIVE BRUSHWORK AND ELEMENTARY DE-
SIGN. A Manual for the Use of Teachers and Students. By
HENRY CADNESS, Second Master of the Municipal School of
Art, Manchester. Second Edition, revised and enlarged, with
upwards of 450 Examples of Design.

"In fact, the very grammar and technique of design is cemented within the compass of this
volume, which is likely to prove a powerful aid to those who propose to devote themselves to
designing, an occupation in which there is a wide and ample field."—*The Queen.*

Large 8vo, cloth. 3s. 6d. net.

SOME TERMS COMMONLY USED IN ORNAMENTAL
DESIGN, their Application Defined and Explained. By
T. ERAT HARRISON and W. G. PAULSON TOWNSEND, Examiners
in Design to the Board of Education. With numerous Illustrations, including many beautiful examples of design.

B. T. BATSFORD,
PUBLISHER,
94, High Holborn, London.

Folio, buckram, gilt. £5 5s. net.

OLD SILVERWORK, CHIEFLY ENGLISH, FROM THE XVth TO THE XVIIIth CENTURIES. A series of choice examples selected from the unique loan collection exhibited at St. James's Court, London, in aid of the funds of the Children's Hospital, supplemented by some further fine specimens from the collections of the Dukes of Devonshire and Rutland. Edited, with Historical and Descriptive Notes, by J. STARKIE GARDNER, F.S.A. Containing 121 beautiful Collotype Plates reproduced in the most effective manner, and illustrating some of the choicest specimens of the Art during the Stuart, Queen Anne, and Georgian periods.

Folio, cloth, gilt. £1 16s. net.

ENGLISH INTERIOR WOODWORK of the XVI., XVII., and XVIII. Centuries. A series of 50 Plates of Drawings to scale and Sketches, chiefly of domestic work, illustrating a fine series of examples of Chimney Pieces, Panelling, Sides of Rooms, Staircases, Doors, Screens, &c., &c., with full practical details and descriptive text. By HENRY TANNER, A.R.I.B.A., Joint Author of "Some Architectural Works of Inigo Jones."

Large 8vo, cloth, gilt. 12s. 6d. net.

THE DECORATION OF HOUSES. A Study of House Decoration during the Renaissance Period, with suggestions for the decorative treatment, furnishing, and arrangement of modern houses. By EDITH WHARTON and OGDEN CODMAN, Architect. With 56 full-page Photographic Illustrations.

"The book is one which should be in the library of every man and woman of means, for its advice is characterised by so much common sense as well as by the best of taste."—*The Queen.*

Large folio, handsomely bound in old style. £1 10s. net.

THE DECORATIVE WORK OF ROBERT AND JAMES ADAM. Being a Reproduction of all the Plates illustrating DECORATION and FURNITURE from their "WORKS IN ARCHITECTURE," published 1778—1812. Containing 30 large folio Plates (size, 19 inches by 14 inches) giving about 100 examples of Rooms, Ceilings, Chimney-pieces, Tables, Chairs, Vases, Lamps, Mirrors, Pier-glasses, Clocks, &c., &c., by these famous Eighteenth-century Designers.

Demy 4to, cloth, gilt. 12s. 6d. net.

PRACTICAL DRAPERY CUTTING. A Handbook on Cutting and Fixing Curtains, Draperies, &c., with descriptions and practical notes, for the use of Upholsterers, Cutters, and Apprentices. By E. NOETZLI, formerly Lecturer and Instructor on Upholstery at the Municipal School of Technology, Manchester. Illustrated by 30 full-page Plates.

Medium 8vo, cloth, gilt. 15s. net.

OLD CLOCKS AND WATCHES AND THEIR MAKERS.
Being an Historical and Descriptive Account of the different
Styles of Clocks and Watches of the Past in England and
Abroad, to which is added a List of 10,000 Makers. By F. J.
BRITTEN. Second edition, much enlarged, containing 740 pages,
with 700 illustrations, mostly reproduced from photographs.

" It is a book which may be augmented in the future, but will scarcely be replaced, and
which holds, in its way, a unique position in literature. . . . To the collector and amateur
it is indispensable."—*Notes and Queries.*

Small folio, cloth, gilt, old style. £2 10s. net.

HEPPLEWHITE'S CABINET-MAKER AND UPHOL-
STERER'S GUIDE; or, Repository of Designs for every article
of Household Furniture in the newest and most approved taste.
A complete facsimile reproduction of this rare work (published
in 1794), containing nearly 300 charming Designs on 128 Plates.

Original copies when met with fetch from £17 *to* £18.

"Hepplewhite's designs are characterised by admirable taste and perfect workmanship. . . .
They are kept clear of the pitfalls which proved so fatal to the reputation of Chippendale, and not
a few of them attain to a standard of refinement beyond which it seems hardly possible to go."—
The Cabinet Maker.

Imperial 8vo, cloth, gilt. 15s. net.

ENGLISH FURNITURE DESIGNERS OF THE XVIIITH
CENTURY. By CONSTANCE SIMON. Containing upwards of
200 pages, with 62 full-page Illustrations of choice and little-
known Specimens, beautifully reproduced in half-tone from
special photographs.

" This is a book of unusual excellence, for which students of Miss Simon's fascinating but
obscure subject will have very good cause to be grateful. So little is known of the lives and
personalities of the great cabinet-makers of the Georgian period that the additions to our knowledge which her industry and research have enabled her to make are not only of substantial value
in themselves, but will entitle her book to a distinguished place in furniture literature. The
illustrations add most appreciably to the value of this well-informed, original, and authoritative
piece of work, in which nothing is slurred over, and nothing taken for granted."—*The Standard.*

Demy 4to, art linen, gilt. £1 5s. net.

COLONIAL FURNITURE IN AMERICA. By LUKE VINCENT
LOCKWOOD. An Historical and Descriptive Handbook of
the Old English and Dutch Furniture, chiefly of the 17th
and 18th Centuries, introduced into America by the Colonists.
With 300 Illustrations of Chests, Couches, Sofas, Tables, Chairs,
Settees, Cupboards, Sideboards, Mirrors, Chests of Drawers,
Bedsteads, Desks, &c.

To collectors, amateurs, and furniture designers this volume cannot but
be of the greatest interest and value, for while much of the furniture
illustrated is of English origin, all the examples are in keeping with the
best traditions of design and workmanship characteristic of English work of
the 17th and 18th centuries.

B. T. BATSFORD,
PUBLISHER,
94, High Holborn, London.

Folio, enclosed in Portfolio. 15s. net.

EXAMPLES OF FURNITURE AND DECORATION DESIGNED BY THOMAS SHERATON. Containing a selection of 167 specimens, reproduced on 16 Plates (18 ins. by 12 ins.), from his rare "Cabinet Maker and Upholsterer's Drawing Book," published 1791—1802.

Folio, cloth, gilt. £2 2s. net.

OLD OAK ENGLISH FURNITURE. A Series of Measured Drawings, with some examples of Architectural Woodwork, Plasterwork, Metalwork, Glazing, &c. By J. W. HURRELL, Architect. Containing 110 full-page Plates.

For ingenuity and quaintness of design, richness of moulding, and profusion of ornament, the old oak furniture of England is probably unsurpassed by the contemporaneous work of any other country. Mr. Hurrell's plates illustrate the true spirit of the work by means of an exhaustive detailed analysis of its construction and design.

Imperial 4to, in cloth portfolio, gilt. £1 8s.

DETAILS OF GOTHIC WOOD-CARVING. Being a series of Drawings from original work of the XIVth and XVth Centuries. By FRANKLYN A. CRALLAN. Containing 34 Photo-lithographic Plates, two of which are double, illustrating some of the finest specimens of Gothic Wood Carving extant. With sections where necessary, and descriptive text.

FRENCH WOOD - CARVINGS FROM THE NATIONAL MUSEUMS. A series of Examples printed in Collotype from Photographs specially taken from the Carvings direct. Edited by ELEANOR ROWE. Part I., Late 15th and Early 16th Century Examples; Part II., 16th Century Work; Part III., 17th and 18th Centuries. The 3 Series complete, each containing 18 large folio Plates, with Descriptive Letterpress, folio, in portfolios, price 12s. each net; or handsomely half-bound in one volume, £2 5s. net.

"This invaluable collection . . . *should be possessed by every carver, both professional and amateur.* . . . The plates are on so large a scale, and are so clearly produced, that they become equivalent, for the purposes of study, to the original works."—*The Architect.*

Demy 8vo, cloth, gilt. 7s. 6d. net.

PRACTICAL WOOD-CARVING. A Book for the Student, Carver, Teacher, Designer, and Architect. By ELEANOR ROWE, twenty years Manager of the School of Art Wood-Carving, Kensington, author of "Hints on Chip-Carving," "French Wood-Carvings," &c. Containing 200 pages of Letterpress, with 114 Illustrations from Photographs and 55 from Line Drawings, showing the Carver at work, examples of Carving in progressive stages of execution, and numerous Illustrations of Old and Modern Carvings.

"Out of the rich stores of many years' knowledge and experience of her subject, Miss Rowe has given to all lovers of this beautiful handicraft a manual of the greatest value. Miss Rowe's long experience of teaching has given her the fullest acquaintance with the needs and difficulties of the carver, and thus her training is based upon a practical sympathy which makes it peculiarly helpful."—*The Queen.*

Imperial 4to, enclosed in strong portfolio. 8s. 6d. net.

OLD ENGLISH WOOD-CARVING PATTERNS. A Collection of Facsimile Rubbings from Oak Furniture of the Jacobean Period. Specially prepared for the use of Teachers, Students, and Classes. By MARGARET F. MALIM. Comprising 30 Examples on 20 Plates (15 ins. × 11 ins.), reproduced by phototint process.

These full-size reproductions of the delightful patterns found on Old English furniture will be invaluable to wood carvers of all classes ; for not only are they exceptionally good from the standpoint of design, but so easy of execution, that amateurs who have attained to but moderate skill in the craft can successfully reproduce them without difficulty.

Imperial 8vo, enclosed in strong portfolio. 6s. net.

WOOD-CARVING DESIGNS. A Series for Students, Teachers, Designers, and Amateurs. By MURIEL MOLLER. With Foreword by WALTER CRANE. Six imperial sheets (31 ins. × 22 ins.), comprising 31 Working Drawings of Panels, Frames, &c., with Photographic Reproductions of the finished work, and 20 designs for Furniture, in which the panels, &c., may be applied.

Crown 8vo, paper covers. 1s.

HINTS ON WOOD - CARVING FOR BEGINNERS. By ELEANOR ROWE. Containing notes on the tools, selection of the wood, and methods of carving, &c. Fourth Edition, revised and enlarged, with 23 full-page and smaller Illustrations.

"The most useful and practical small book on wood-carving we know of."—*The Builder.*
" Full of sound directions and good suggestions."—*The Magazine of Art.*

Crown 8vo, paper covers. 1s.

HINTS ON CHIP-CARVING and Simple Northern Styles. Containing practical instructions on the setting out of the patterns, on the use of the tools, and the methods of carving. By ELEANOR ROWE. With 40 Illustrations.

" A capital manual of instruction in a craft that ought to be most popular."—*Saturday Review.*

Imperial folio, buckram, gilt. £3 3s. net.

ENGLISH AND SCOTTISH WROUGHT IRONWORK. A Series of Examples of English Ironwork of the best period, with which is included most that now exists in Scotland. By BAILEY SCOTT MURPHY, Architect. Containing 80 fine Plates (size 21½ ins. by 14½ ins.), 68 reproduced from measured drawings, and 12 from photographs specially taken. With Descriptive Text.

" This volume stands alone as a unique collection of the best work in wrought iron done in Great Britain. It is replete with exact delineations and precise dimensions technically and thoroughly realised for the student and practical craftsman."—*The Building News.*

Demy 8vo, cloth. 6s.

A HANDBOOK OF ART SMITHING. By F. S. MEYER, Author of " A Handbook of Ornament." With an Introduction by J. STARKIE GARDNER. Containing 214 Illustrations.

" A most excellent manual, crowded with examples of ancient work. The Introduction is by Mr. Starkie Gardner, and students know what that name implies."—*The Studio.*

B. T. BATSFORD,
PUBLISHER,
94, High Holborn, London.

Large Imperial 8vo, cloth.   7s. 6d. net.

ARCHITECTURAL SKETCHING AND DRAWING IN PER-
SPECTIVE. A Progressive Series of 36 Plates, illustrating
the Drawing of Architectural Details, and Sketching to Scale ;
with Chapters on Various Perspective Methods. Figures, Foliage,
&c. Based to some extent on R.'s Method of Perspective.
By H. W. ROBERTS, Author of " R.'s Method."

Demy 8vo, cloth.   2s. 6d. net.

THE PRINCIPLES OF ARCHITECTURAL PERSPECTIVE.
Prepared for the Use of Students, &c., with chapters on Iso-
metric Drawing and the Preparation of Finished Perspectives.
By G. A. T. MIDDLETON, A.R.I.B.A. Illustrated with 51
Diagrams and 8 finished Drawings by various Architects.

Crown 8vo, art linen.   5s. 6d. net.

PEN DRAWING. AN ILLUSTRATED TREATISE. By CHARLES D.
MAGINNIS, Instructor in Pen Drawing, Boston Architectural
Club. With a special chapter on Architectural Drawing. Illus-
trated by 72 Reproductions of the Work of the principal
Black-and-White Artists, Practical Diagrams, &c.

Large 8vo, art linen.   7s. 6d. net.

THE APPRECIATION OF PICTURES. An Historical and
Critical Handbook of Ancient and Modern Art for the Artist,
Student, and Connoisseur. By RUSSELL STURGIS, M.A. With
73 full-page Photographs after Famous Pictures.

" This book is so well founded in the study of the masters, old and new ; so faithful to the
true idea of the graphic arts, and so well written, that it could be read with interest and sympathy
by anybody who loves paint."—*The Scotsman.*

Large 8vo, art linen.   7s. 6d. net.

PICTORIAL   COMPOSITION   AND   THE   CRITICAL
JUDGMENT OF PICTURES. A Handbook for Students
and lovers of Art. By H. R. POORE. With about 150 Illustrations, chiefly reproduced from photographs, of celebrated
pictures, including numerous elucidatory diagrams.

One of the best works of its kind. Of particular value to the artist, to
the art student, and to all interested in understanding the merits of a picture.
The book is, in fact, a liberal education in art.

Large 8vo, cloth, gilt.   12s. 6d. net.

ART PRINCIPLES IN PORTRAIT PHOTOGRAPHY: Composition; Treatment of Backgrounds, and the Processes involved
in Manipulating the Plate. By OTTO WALTER BECK. With
138 full-page and smaller illustrations, reproduced from specially
taken photographs and original diagrams.

" The book deals very ably with the limitations and with the possibilities of the camera in
portraiture. Too often the photographer has neither received any serious artistic training nor
had the opportunity for intelligent study. While I do not think there is any short cut to success
in Pictorial Portraiture, the book cannot fail to be most helpful and conducive to good if followed
out."—MR. FURLEY LEWIS, F.R.P.S.

3 vols., large folio, strongly bound in buckram, gilt. £15 15s. net.

MODERN OPERA-HOUSES AND THEATRES. Examples of Playhouses recently erected in Europe. With Descriptive Accounts, a Treatise on Theatre Planning and Construction, and Supplements on Stage Machinery, Theatre Fires, and Protective Legislation. By EDWIN O. SACHS, Architect. Complete in Three Grand Folio Volumes, containing over 200 large Folio Plates, reproduced in the best manner by Photo-lithography, and some 600 Diagrams, interspersed in the 350 pages of Text.

" Mr. Sachs has given us a work which most usefully and adequately fills a gap in architectural literature."—*The British Architect.*
"The undertaking surpasses anything of the kind ever attempted in this country." *The Building News.*

Crown 4to, cloth, gilt. 5s. net.

THE ST. LOUIS EXHIBITION, 1904. An Illustrated Account of the Exhibition and its Buildings. By H. PHILLIPS FLETCHER, F.R.I.B.A. Containing 43 full-page and smaller Illustrations of plans, sections, elevations, and details of construction of the various buildings.

Square 8vo, cloth, gilt. 6s. net.

FARM BUILDINGS: THEIR CONSTRUCTION AND ARRANGEMENT. By A. DUDLEY CLARKE, F.S.I. 3rd Edition, revised and much enlarged. With chapters on Cottages, Homesteads, Roofs, Sanitary Matters, &c. Containing 52 Plates, and many other Illustrations.

Adopted as the text-book by the Surveyors' Institution.
Mr. Clarke's handbook is the best of its kind."—*The Surveyor.*

2 vols., crown 8vo, cloth, gilt. 7s. 6d.

CONCRETE: ITS USE IN BUILDING. A Practical Handbook dealing with Walls, Paving, Roofs, Floors, and other details of Concrete Construction. By THOS. POTTER. Second Edition, greatly enlarged, containing 500 pages with 100 Illustrations.

Large 8vo, cloth, gilt. 8s. 6d. net.

THE PRINCIPLES OF PLANNING. By PERCY L. MARKS, Architect. With Notes on the Essential Features and Requirements of Different Classes of Buildings. Illustrated by 150 Plans, mainly of important modern Buildings. Second Edition, revised and greatly enlarged.

"It will be found a suggestive and useful book on the subject."—*The British Architect.*

Imperial 8vo, cloth, gilt. 12s. 6d. net.

PUBLIC LIBRARIES: A Treatise on their Design, Construction, and Fittings, with a Chapter on the Principles of Planning, and a Summary of the Law. By AMIAN L. CHAMPNEYS, B.A., Architect. Containing about 200 pages, with over 100 Illustrations of Modern Examples and Fittings from Photographs and Drawings.

B. T. BATSFORD,
PUBLISHER,
94, High Holborn, London.

Imperial 8vo, cloth, gilt. £1 5s. net.

MODERN SCHOOL BUILDINGS, ELEMENTARY AND SECONDARY. A Treatise on the Planning, Arrangement, and Fitting of Day and Boarding Schools. With special chapters on the Treatment of Class-rooms, Lighting, Warming, Ventilation, and Sanitation. By FELIX CLAY, B.A., Architect. Second Edition, revised and much enlarged, consisting of 560 pp., with 450 Illustrations of plans, perspective views, constructive details, and fittings.

"Mr. Clay's book is an eminently practical one, illustrated by actually executed examples. It is full of valuable information carefully arranged, and the author is to be congratulated on the production of a work which should at once take rank as the standard authority on the subject."— *The Architectural Review.*

Imperial 8vo, cloth, gilt. 21s. net.

RESIDENTIAL FLATS OF ALL CLASSES, INCLUDING ARTISANS' DWELLINGS. A Practical Treatise on their Planning and Arrangement, together with chapters on their History, Financial Matters, &c. By SYDNEY PERKS, F.R.I.B.A., P.A.S.I. Containing 300 pages, with 226 Illustrations, including plans and views of important Examples by leading architects in England, the Continent, and America.

"The great monograph of the year (1905) was Mr. Perks' book on the planning of flats—a standard work of considerable importance."—*The Building News.*

Imperial 8vo, cloth, gilt. 21s. net.

PUBLIC BATHS AND WASH-HOUSES. A Treatise on their Planning, Design, Arrangement, and Fitting, with chapters on Turkish, Russian and other special Baths, Public Laundries, Engineering, Heating, Water Supply, &c. By A. W. S. CROSS, M.A., F.R.I.B.A. Containing about 300 pages, with 274 Illustrations of modern examples.

Crown 4to, cloth, gilt. 15s. net.

THE COUNTRY HOUSE. A practical Manual of the Planning and Construction of the American Country Home and its Surroundings. By C. E. HOOPER. With about 400 Illustrations, comprising Photographic Views, Plans, Constructive and Ornamental Details, &c.

To those contemplating the building of a country house, this volume will be of the greatest service. It contains advice and hints on every essential point, including the selection of the site, the planning and arrangement of the structure, the practical details of construction and sanitation, the decoration of the interior, and the laying-out of the garden.

Imperial 4to, cloth, gilt. £1 1s. net.

A BOOK OF COUNTRY HOUSES. Containing 62 Plates reproduced from Photographs and Drawings of Perspective Views and Plans of a variety of executed examples, ranging in size from a moderate-sized Suburban House to a fairly large Mansion. By ERNEST NEWTON, Architect.

The houses illustrated in this volume have been planned during the last ten years, and may be taken as representative of the English Country House of the present day. They offer much variety in their size, their sites, the character of the materials in which they are constructed, and their types of plan.

Demy 4to, cloth, gilt. 10s. 6d. *net.*

HOMES FOR THE COUNTRY. A Collection of Designs and Examples of recently executed works. By R. A. BRIGGS, Architect, F.R.I.B.A., Soane Medallist. Containing 48 full-page Plates of Exterior and Interior Views and Plans. With descriptive notes.

"Every example given is an illustration of very considerable skill. The plans are all excellent—well devised on ecoromical yet convenient lines, well lit, comfortable, and with every little point thought out ; while the elevations are pleasing without being extravagant. Such a book is admirable in its suggestiveness, and useful to all."—*The Architect's Magazine.*

Demy 4to, cloth, gilt. 12s. 6d.

BUNGALOWS AND COUNTRY RESIDENCES. A Series of Designs and Examples of executed Works. By R. A. BRIGGS, F.R.I.B.A. 5th and enlarged Edition, containing 47 Photolithographic Plates, with descriptive notes and particulars of cost.

"Those who desire grace and originality in their suburban dwellings might take many a valuable hint from this book."—*The Times.*

Royal 4to, cloth, gilt. 10s. 6d. *net.*

MODERN COTTAGE ARCHITECTURE, illustrated from Works of well-known Architects. Edited, with an Essay on Cottage Building, and descriptive notes on the subjects, by MAURICE B. ADAMS, F.R.I.B.A. Containing 50 Plates of Perspective Views and Plans of the best types of country cottages.

"The cottages which Mr. Adams has selected would do credit to any estate in England."— *The Architect.*

Imperial 4to, cloth, gilt. £1 1s. *net.*

HOUSES FOR THE WORKING CLASSES. Comprising 52 Typical and Improved Plans, with Elevations, Details, &c., and Descriptive Text, including Notes on the Treatment and Planning of Small Houses. By S. W. CRANFIELD and H. I. POTTER, AA.R.I.B.A. Second Edition, revised and enlarged.

This book deals with Cottages suitable for the Working Classes in Suburban and Rural Districts. The majority of the examples illustrated consist of two and three-storey dwellings, adapted to be built in pairs, groups, or terraces, and vary in cost from £160 to £650.

Royal 4to, cloth, gilt. 7s. 6d. *net.*

MODERN HOUSING IN TOWN AND COUNTRY. Illustrated by examples of municipal and other schemes of Block Dwellings, Tenement Houses, Model Cottages and Villages, and the Garden City, together with Illustrations of the Cheap Cottages Exhibition. By JAMES CORNES. With many Plans and Views from Drawings and Photographs. Full Descriptive Text and particulars of Cost, &c.

Large 4to, art linen, gilt. 16s. *net.*

MODERN SUBURBAN HOUSES. A Series of Examples erected at Hampstead, Bickley, and in Surrey, from the designs of C. H. B. QUENNELL, Architect. Containing 44 Plates, consisting of Exterior and Interior Views, reproduced from special photographs, and large-scale plans, from the author's drawings.

B. T. BATSFORD,
PUBLISHER,
94, High Holborn, London.

Crown 4to, cloth. 12s. 6d. net.

MODERN PRACTICAL CARPENTRY. For the use of Workmen, Builders, Architects, and Engineers. By GEORGE ELLIS, author of "Modern Practical Joinery," &c. Containing a full description of the Methods of Constructing and Erecting Roofs, Floors, Partitions, Scaffolding, Shoring, Centering, Stands and Stages, Coffer Dams, Foundations, Bridges, Gates, Tunnels, Excavations, Wood and Half-timber Houses, and various Structural Details. Together with new and simple methods of finding the Bevels in Roofs, Setting-out Domes, Steeples, &c., a concise Treatise on Timber, Notes on the Woods used, a Glossary of Technical Terms and Phrases, and a chapter on the Uses of the Steel Square. 450 pages, with 1,100 clear and practical Illustrations.

"A handsome and substantial volume. The product has been well carried out. It excels nearly all in its completeness. There is a large number of clear detailed drawings. The production of the work is worthy of the excellence of the subject-matter."—*The Carpenter and Builder.*

"The book is full of sound, practical matter. It is profusely illustrated with the clearest of line drawings and photographs, not mere sketches, but working drawings of the highest possible value. Anyone confronted with an unusual difficulty would almost surely find its solution somewhere in the volume."—*The Building News.*

Crown 4to, cloth. 12s. 6d. net.

MODERN PRACTICAL JOINERY. A Treatise on the Practice of Joiner's Work by Hand and Machine. By GEORGE ELLIS. Containing a full Description of Hand-tools and their Uses, Workshop Practice, Fittings and Appliances, the Preparation of all kinds of House Joinery, Bank, Office, Church, Museum and Shop-fittings, Air-tight Cases, and Shaped Work. With concise Treatises on Stair-building and Hand-railing, and a Glossary of Terms, &c. 380 pages, with 1,000 practical Illustrations.

"In this excellent work the mature fruits of the first-hand practical experience of an exceptionally skilful and intelligent craftsman are given. It is a credit to the author's talent and industry, and is likely to remain an enduring monument to British craftsmanship. As a standard work it will doubtless be adopted and esteemed by the architect, builder, and the aspiring workman."—*The Building World.*

Large 8vo, cloth, gilt. 5s. net.

SCAFFOLDING: A Treatise on the Design and Erection of Scaffolds, Gantries, and Stagings, with an Account of the Appliances used in connection therewith, and a Chapter on the Legal Aspect of the Question. By A. G. H. THATCHER, Surveyor. With 146 Diagrams and 6 full-page Plates.

Demy 4to, cloth. 18s. net.

PLASTERING—PLAIN AND DECORATIVE. A Practical Treatise on the Art and Craft of Plastering and Modelling. Including full descriptions of the various Tools, Materials, Processes, and Appliances employed, and important chapters on Concrete Work. By WILLIAM MILLAR. With an Introduction by G. T. ROBINSON, F.S.A., treating of the History of Art. Containing 600 pages of text, with 550 Illustrations. Third Edition, revised and enlarged.

Large crown 8vo, cloth, gilt. 10s. *net.*

BUILDING MATERIALS: THEIR NATURE, PROPERTIES, AND MANUFACTURE. A Text-book for Students. By G. A. T. MIDDLETON, Architect, A.R.I.B.A., Author of "Stresses and Thrusts," "Drainage," &c. Containing 450 pages of Text, with 200 Illustrations from specially prepared drawings, and 12 full-page Photographic Plates.

This work contains a *résumé* of the latest and most reliable information on the subject, presented in a clear and concise way.

Crown 8vo, cloth, gilt. 3s.

BUILDING CONSTRUCTION AND DRAWING. A TEXT-BOOK ON THE PRINCIPLES AND DETAILS OF MODERN CONSTRUCTION. For the Use of Students and Practical Men. By CHARLES F. MITCHELL, assisted by GEORGE A. MITCHELL, Lecturers on Building Construction at the Polytechnic Institute, London. FIRST STAGE OR ELEMENTARY COURSE. 7th Edition (70th Thousand), revised and greatly enlarged. Containing 470 pages of Text, with 1,100 Illustrations, fully dimensioned.

"The book is a model of clearness and compression, well written and admirably illustrated, and ought to be in the hands of every student of building construction."—*The Builder.*

Crown 8vo, cloth, gilt. 5s. 6d.

BUILDING CONSTRUCTION. A TEXT-BOOK ON THE PRINCIPLES AND DETAILS OF MODERN CONSTRUCTION. By CHARLES F. MITCHELL, assisted by GEORGE A. MITCHELL. (ADVANCED AND HONOURS COURSES.) For the use of Students preparing for the Examinations of the Board of Education, the Royal Institute of British Architects, the Surveyors' Institution, the City Guilds, &c., and for those engaged in building. Containing 800 pages of Text, with over 750 Illustrations, fully dimensioned. 5th Edition (33rd Thousand), thoroughly revised and much enlarged.

"Mr. Mitchell's two books form unquestionably the best guide which any student can obtain at the present moment. In fact, so far as it is possible for anyone to compile a satisfactory treatise on building construction, Mr. Mitchell has performed the task as well as it can be performed."—*The Builder.*

Crown 8vo, cloth, gilt. 5s.

BRICKWORK AND MASONRY. A Practical Text-book for Students and those engaged in the Design and Execution of Structures in Brick and Stone. By CHARLES F. MITCHELL, assisted by GEORGE A. MITCHELL. Being a thoroughly revised and remodelled edition of the chapters on these subjects from the authors' "Elementary" and "Advanced Building Construction," with special additional chapters and new illustrations. 400 pp., with about 600 Illustrations (fully dimensioned), including numerous full and double-page Plates.

"Regarded in its entirety, this is a most valuable work. It is not a treatise, as the term is generally understood, but a compendium of useful information admirably collated and well illustrated, and as such has a distinct sphere of usefulness."—*The Builder.*

B. T. BATSFORD,
PUBLISHER,
94, High Holborn, London.

Large thick 8vo, cloth, gilt. 18s. net.

BUILDING SPECIFICATIONS for the use of Architects, Surveyors, Builders, &c. Comprising the complete Specification of a large House, with Stables, Conservatory, &c.; also numerous Clauses relating to Special Classes of Buildings, and Practical Notes on all Trades and Sections. By JOHN LEANING, F.S.I., Author of "Quantity Surveying," &c. Containing 630 pages of Text, with 140 Illustrations. The most comprehensive, systematic, and practical treatise on the subject.

" A very valuable book on this subject, and one which must become a standard work in relation thereto. . . . Mr. Leaning has thoroughly mastered his subject in all its intricacy of detail, and in dealing with it is clear, concise, and definite."—*The Architect.*

Large 8vo, cloth, gilt. 4s. 6d.

TREATISE ON SHORING AND UNDERPINNING, and generally dealing with dangerous Structures. By C. H. STOCK. Third Edition, revised and enlarged by F. R. FARROW, F.R.I.B.A. With 40 clear and practical Illustrations.

" Mr. Stock has supplied a manifest want in the literature of practical architecture and surveying, and there is no doubt his book will be of great practical use."—*The Builder.*

Crown 8vo, cloth, gilt. 4s. 6d. net.

STRESSES AND THRUSTS. A Text-book on their Determination in Constructional Work, with Examples of the Design of Girders and Roofs, for the use of Students. By G. A. T. MIDDLETON, A.R.I.B.A. Third Edition, thoroughly revised and much enlarged. With 170 illustrative Diagrams and Folding Plates.

" The student of building construction will find in this book all he ought to know as to the relation of stresses and thrusts to the work he may be engaged in. Foundations, chimneys, walls, roofs, steel joists, girders, stanchions, are all taken in detail, and the varying degrees of stress are calculated in a simple way, so that the merest tyro in mathematics will be able to appreciate and apply the principles laid down."—*The Surveyor.*

Crown 8vo, cloth, gilt. 3s. net.

THE ELEMENTARY PRINCIPLES OF GRAPHIC STATICS. Specially prepared for the Use of Students entering for the Examinations in Building Construction, Applied Mechanics, Machine Construction and Drawing, &c., of the Board of Education. By EDWARD HARDY, Teacher of Building Construction. Illustrated by 150 clear Diagrams.

Prof. **Henry Adams**, writing to the Author, says :—" You have treated the subject in a very clear and logical manner, and I shall certainly recommend the book to my elementary students as the best of its kind."

Small 8vo, cloth, gilt. 2s. 6d. net.

THE CONDUCT OF BUILDING WORK AND THE DUTIES OF A CLERK OF WORKS. A Handy Guide to the Superintendence of Building Operations. By J. LEANING, F.S.I. Second Edition, revised and enlarged.

" This most admirable little volume should be read by all those who have charge of building operations . . . . In a concise form it deals with many of the important points arising during the erection of a building."—*The British Architect.*

Large crown 8vo, cloth, gilt.   7s. 6d. net.

HOW TO ESTIMATE : OR THE ANALYSIS OF BUILDERS'
PRICES. A Complete Guide to the Practice of Estimating,
and a Reference Book of the most reliable Building Prices.
By JOHN T. REA, F.S.I., Surveyor, War Department.
With typical examples in each trade, and a large amount of
useful information for the guidance of Estimators, including
thousands of prices.   Second Edition, revised and enlarged.

" Here at last is a book that can be confidently recommended as a comprehensive, practical,
trustworthy, cheap, and really modern book on estimating. The book is excellent in plan,
thorough in execution, clear in exposition, and will be a boon alike to the raw student and to
the experienced estimator. For the former it will be an invaluable instructor ; for the
latter a trustworthy remembrancer and an indispensable work of reference."—*The Building
World.*

Crown 8vo, cloth, gilt.   4s. 6d. net.

ESTIMATING. A Method of Pricing Builders' Quantities for
Competitive Work, without the use of a Price Book. By
GEORGE STEPHENSON.   6th Edition, the Prices carefully revised.

" Mr. Stephenson has succeeded in removing many of the difficulties in this branch of his
profession, and anyone who has mastered this little book will be enabled to price a bill of
quantities without recourse to his Laxton."—*The Building News.*

Crown 8vo, cloth, gilt.   3s. net.

REPAIRS : HOW TO MEASURE AND VALUE THEM. A
Handbook for the use of Builders, Decorators, &c.   By the
Author of " Estimating," &c.   4th Edition, revised to date.

" ' Repairs' is a very serviceable handbook on the subject. The author proceeds, from the
top floor downwards, to show how to value the items, by a method of framing the estimate in the
measuring book. The *modus operandi* is simple and soon learnt."—*The Building News.*

Crown 8vo, cloth, gilt.   3s. 6d. net.

THE QUANTITY STUDENT'S ASSISTANT. A Handbook of
Practical Notes and Memoranda for those learning to take-off
Quantities.   By GEORGE STEPHENSON, Author of " Repairs,"&c.

Large crown 8vo, cloth, gilt.   5s. net.

GASFITTING. A Practical Handbook relating to the Distribution
of Gas in Service Pipes, the Use of Coal Gas, and the best
Means of Economising Gas from Main to Burner.   By WALTER
GRAFTON, F.C.S., Chemist at the Beckton Works of the Gas
Light and Coke Co.   With 143 Illustrations.

" The author is a recognised authority upon the subject of gas-lighting, and gas-fitters and
others who intend to study gas-fitting in practical detail will find the book most serviceable."—
The Builder.

Large 8vo, cloth, gilt.   4s. 6d. net.

THE DRAINAGE OF TOWN AND COUNTRY HOUSES.
A Practical Account of Modern Sanitary Arrangements and
Fittings.   By G. A. T. MIDDLETON, A.R.I.B.A.   With full
particulars of the latest fittings and arrangements, and a special
chapter on the Disposal of Sewage on a small scale, including
an account of the Bacterial Method.   With 90 Illustrations.

B.   T.   BATSFORD,
PUBLISHER,
94, High Holborn, London.

Thick royal 8vo, cloth, gilt. 12s. 6d.

THE PLUMBER AND SANITARY HOUSES. A Practical Treatise on the Principles of Internal Plumbing Work; or the best means for effectually excluding Noxious Gases from our Houses. By S. STEVENS HELLYER. 6th Edition, revised and enlarged. With 30 Plates, and 262 Woodcut Illustrations.

"The best treatise existing on Practical Plumbing."—*The Builder.*
"This work is an exhaustive treatise on the subject of House Sanitation, comprising all that relates to Drainage, Ventilation, and Water Supply within and appertaining to the house."—*The Journal of the Royal Institute of British Architects.*

Large thick 8vo, cloth, gilt. £1 12s. net.

SANITARY ENGINEERING. A Compendium of the latest and most reliable information on Sanitary Science in all its branches. By Colonel E. C. S. MOORE, R.E., M.S.I. Second Edition, thoroughly revised and greatly enlarged. Containing 830 pp. of Text, with 860 Illustrations, including 92 large Folding Plates.

". . . A full and complete epitome of the latest practice in sanitary engineering. . . AS A BOOK OF REFERENCE IT IS SIMPLY INDISPENSABLE."—*The Public Health Engineer.*
". . . We know of no single volume which contains such a mass of well-arranged information. It is encyclopædic, and should take its place as the standard book on the wide and important subject with which it deals."—*The Surveyor.*

Large 8vo, cloth, gilt. 6s. net.

WATERWORKS DISTRIBUTION. A Practical Guide to the Laying Out of Systems of distributing Mains for the Supply of Water to Cities and Towns. By J. A. McFHERSON, M.Inst.C.E. Second Edition, revised and enlarged, fully illustrated by 130 Diagrams.

"The author has evidently a large practical experience of the subject on which he has written, and he has succeeded in compiling a book which is sure to take its place among the standard works on water supply."—*The Surveyor.*

Large 8vo, cloth. 3s. 6d. net.

TECHNICAL PLUMBING. A Handbook for Students and Practical Men. By S. BARLOW BENNETT, Lecturer on Sanitary Engineering to the Durham County Council. Second Edition, revised, with about 500 Illustrations.

Small pocket size, leather, 1s. 6d. net, *or in celluloid case* 2s. net.

CLARKE'S POCKET-BOOK OF TABLES AND MEMO-RANDA FOR PLUMBERS, BUILDERS, SANITARY AND ELECTRICAL ENGINEERS, &c. By J. WRIGHT CLARKE, M.S.I. With a new Section of Electrical Memoranda and Formulæ. Entirely New and Revised Edition.

"It is obviously one of those things a tradesman should carry in his pocket as religiously as he does a foot rule."—*The Plumber and Decorator.*
"The amount of information this excellent little work contains is marvellous."—*The Sanitary Record.*

Large 8vo, cloth, gilt. 5s. net.

PRACTICAL SCIENCE FOR PLUMBERS. By J. WRIGHT CLARKE. Treating of Physics, Metals, Hydraulics, Heat, Temperature, &c., and their application to the problems of practical work. With about 200 Illustrations.

Crown 8vo, cloth, gilt. 3s. 6d. net.

PUMPS: THEIR PRINCIPLES AND CONSTRUCTION.
A Series of Lectures delivered at the Regent Street Polytechnic, London. By J. WRIGHT CLARKE, Author of "Plumbing Practice." With 73 Illustrations. Second Edition, thoroughly revised, with all the Illustrations specially re-drawn.

Crown 8vo, cloth, gilt. 2s:

HYDRAULIC RAMS: THEIR PRINCIPLES AND CONSTRUCTION.
By J. WRIGHT CLARKE, Author of "Pumps," "Plumbing Practice," &c. With results of Experiments carried out by the Author at the Regent Street Polytechnic and in various parts of the Country. Illustrated by 36 Diagrams.

Crown 8vo, cloth, gilt. 5s. net.

ARCHITECTURAL HYGIENE, or Sanitary Science as applied
to Building. By BANISTER F. FLETCHER, F.R.I.B.A., F.S.I., and H. PHILLIPS FLETCHER, F.R.I.B.A., F.S.I. Second Edition, revised. With upwards of 300 Illustrations.

Royal 8vo, cloth, gilt. 15s. net.

CONDITIONS OF CONTRACT relating to Building Works.
By FRANK W. MACEY, Architect. Revised, as to the strictly legal matter, by B. J. LEVERSON, Barrister-at-Law.

PROFESSOR BANISTER FLETCHER'S VALUABLE TEXT-BOOKS FOR ARCHITECTS AND SURVEYORS.

Arranged in Tabulated Form and fully indexed for ready reference.

Crown 8vo, cloth, gilt. 7s. 6d.

QUANTITIES.
A Text-book explanatory of the Best Methods adopted in the Measurement and Valuation of Builders' Work. 7th Edition, revised throughout and much improved by H. PHILLIPS FLETCHER, F.R.I.B.A., F.S.I. With special chapters on Cubing, Priced Schedules, Grouping, the Law, &c., and a typical example of the complete Taking-off, Abstracting, and Billing in all Trades. Containing about 450 pages, with 10 folding Plates and 100 other Diagrams in the Text.

"It is no doubt the best work on the subject extant."—*The Builder.*
"We compliment Mr. Phillips Fletcher on his revision, and on the accuracy of the book generally."—*The Surveyor.*
"A safe, comprehensive, and concise text-book on an important technical subject. We imagine few surveyors' or architects' shelves will be without it."—*The British Architect.*
"One of the most complete works upon the subject. Of great assistance to students."—*The Builder's Journal.*
"A good treatise by a competent master of the subject."—*The Building News.*

B. T. BATSFORD,
PUBLISHER,
94, High Holborn, London.

PROFESSOR BANISTER FLETCHER'S VALUABLE TEXT-BOOKS FOR ARCHITECTS AND SURVEYORS.

Arranged in Tabulated Form and fully indexed for ready reference.

THE NEW EDITIONS, REVISED AND BROUGHT UP TO DATE
By BANISTER F. FLETCHER, F.R.I.B.A., F.S.I., and
H. PHILLIPS FLETCHER, F.R.I.B.A., F.S.I., Barrister-at-Law.

Crown 8vo, uniformly bound in cloth, gilt. 6s. 6d. each.

LONDON BUILDING ACTS, 1894-1905. A Text-book on the Law relating to Building in the Metropolis. Containing the Acts *in extenso*, the By-laws and Regulations now in force, notes on the Acts, and reports of the principal cases. Fourth Edition, revised. Illustrated by 23 Coloured Plates. Including the full text of the Amendment Act of 1905, with a Note explaining its effect on new and existing buildings.

"IT IS THE LAW OF BUILDING FOR LONDON IN ONE VOLUME."—*The Architect.*
"Illustrated by a series of invaluable coloured plates, showing clearly the meaning of the various clauses as regards construction."—*The Surveyor.*

DILAPIDATIONS. A Text-book on the Law and Practice. 6th Edition, thoroughly revised and enlarged, with the addition of all the most recent Acts and a large number of Legal Decisions, including a chapter on Fixtures.

"An excellent compendium on the law and practice on the subject."—*The Builder.*

LIGHT AND AIR. With Methods of Estimating Injuries, Reports of most recent Cases, &c. Illustrated by 27 Coloured Plates. 4th Edition, revised and enlarged, with an Appendix containing a *résumé* of the House of Lords' decision in the case of "Colls *v.* Home and Colonial Stores."

"By far the most complete and practical text-book we have seen. In it will be found the cream of all the legal definitions and decisions."—*The Building News.*

VALUATIONS AND COMPENSATIONS. A Text-book on the Practice of Valuing Property, and the Law of Compensation in relation thereto. Third Edition revised and enlarged. With an Appendix of Forms of Precedents and an extensive series of Valuation Tables.

"Very useful to students preparing for the examination of the Surveyors' Institution."—*The Surveyor.*
"A complete guide to valuing land and houses for mortgage, renting, or investment, as well as for making valuations, when lands and houses are taken under compulsory powers by public bodies or companies. The tables contained in the Appendix are especially valuable, and there is an exhaustive index."—*The Property Market Review.*

Crown 8vo, cloth, gilt. 5s. 6d.

ARBITRATIONS. A Text-book for Arbitrators, Umpires, and all connected with Arbitrations, more especially Architects, Engineers, and Surveyors, in tabulated form, with the chief cases governing the same, and an Appendix of Forms, Statutes, Rules, &c. Third Edition, revised and largely re-written.

"Especially useful to young surveyors as a compendium of the knowledge which professional experience gives in more concrete form and with infinite variety of detail."—*The Surveyor.*

B. T. BATSFORD, Publisher, 94, High Holborn, London.

DATE DUE

NOV 0 1 1986	OCT 1 1986		

Lightning Source UK Ltd.
Milton Keynes UK
UKHW020020100223
416721UK00002B/338